Happy Birthday
Shirley

Love & Best Wishes

Shirley Lallent

A Taste
for all Seasons

Beverley Sutherland Smith

GALLERY BOOKS
An Imprint of W. H. Smith Publishers Inc.
112 Madison Avenue
New York, New York 10016

A Taste for all Seasons

This edition published 1984 by Gallery Books,
an imprint of W.H. Smith Publishers Inc,
112 Madison Avenue, New York, NY 10016.

ISBN 0-8317-8644-2

Printed and bound in Hong Kong by South China Printing Co.

Contents

Introduction

The recipes in this book were inspired by the most basic part of my cooking life: the trips to the local markets. Here, the kaleidoscope of colour piled up on the stalls and the aroma of fresh vegetables and herbs are a constant and ever-changing source of inspiration.

Freshly picked shiny baby zucchini, violet and green figs, the first pale green asparagus, the perfume of early raspberries, fennel hanging with feathery fronds, the long woven strands of garlic, shiny-eyed fish heaped on ice or plump chickens and quail are a delight to the senses.

Too often, menus are planned in advance at home, when ideally a menu should be chosen after the shopping is finished and the baskets are un-loaded, using ingredients at their peak. Seasonal shopping is the most sensible of all; the finest food doesn't depend on exotic ingredients but on their quality and freshness.

This book follows the seasons. Although some ingredients can be bought all through the year, the styles of dishes are also determined by the weather. They are light and fresh in spring, easy to cook and tempting in summer, slightly heavier for chill autumn winds and nights, and substantial for the winter with a few festive ideas for entertaining.

There are some quick and simple dishes in the book, useful in emergencies, as well as more elaborate recipes for entertaining. The reliance on fresh produce is the common factor with them all. I firmly believe it's the only way to produce good food, surely the aim of people who love cooking.

Spring

ASPARAGUS

This member of the lily family which dates back to Ancient Greece is the first indication in the shops that spring is beginning. Said to cure toothaches, bee stings and all number of ills, we appreciate it now for mainly its delicate flavour. The first few bunches are usually enjoyed just covered with melted butter or hollandaise sauce, then as the season continues, it can be tried in a number of interesting ways.

BASIC PREPARATION: When buying, remember fat spears are just as tender as thin ones and usually less wasteful. With a small sharp knife (or vegetable peeler), peel up the stalk until you come near to the tip. Shave off any scales under the tip and wash. This way the asparagus retains its colour and texture and can be eaten all the way down. Tie in bundles and try and keep them about the same length. Cook in plenty of salted boiling water. Special pans can be bought but unless you grow asparagus or eat huge quantities, the cost of a special pan would hardly be justified. Alternatively, it is best to use a large saucepan and lie them horizontally. Cook until just tender and test by piercing with a sharp knife. They shouldn't be limp when served. Drain well.

Asparagus Vinaigrette à la Crême

This makes enough sauce to cover about 1 kg (2 lb) asparagus spears. Cook asparagus and drain well. Leave to cool and then cover with the sauce. It can be prepared several hours before serving.

Sauce
½ cup cream
2 teaspoons French mustard
1 tablespoon white vinegar
(the best one to use is a tarragon flavoured white wine vinegar)
1 tablespoon mayonnaise
a little salt
white pepper

To Decorate
2 hard boiled eggs
little finely chopped parsley

Whip the cream lightly. Mix in the French mustard, white vinegar and mayonnaise. Season to taste. Spread this in a layer over the stalks of asparagus. Cut the eggs in half. Remove yolks. Chop the whites very finely and push the yolks through a sieve or chop. Arrange a layer of egg white, then yolk and sprinkle a thin line of parsley between.
Serve cold.

Asparagus in Brandy Cream Sauce

The sauce makes enough for 1 kg (2 lb) asparagus
The asparagus can be cooked beforehand, drained well and then kept refrigerated. It reheats successfully in the sauce without losing any flavour.

60 g (2 oz) butter
3 tablespoons brandy
½ cup cream
a little salt
white pepper

Melt the butter and add asparagus. Cook gently until it is warmed through. Add brandy and light. Leave to burn away and then pour over cream. Season with salt and pepper and simmer a minute until the cream has thickened slightly.
This is delicious as an entrée or goes well with a plain chicken dish.

Asparagus Tart

250 g (½ lb) puff pastry
1 flan tin, 23 cm (9 inch)

Roll out puff pastry thinly. Fit into flan tin. Prick the base and line with a little greaseproof paper. Fill with beans or rice and bake in a moderate oven, 180-190°C (350-375°F), until the shell is set. Remove beans and cook another couple of minutes to dry out. Be careful not to overcook at this stage as it will go back in the oven with the filling.

Filling
60 g (2 oz) butter
1 large white onion, finely diced
125 g (¼ lb) mushrooms, diced roughly
½ cup chopped ham
500 g (1 lb) asparagus, cooked and drained well
2 eggs
¾ cup cream
salt and pepper

Melt the butter and cook onion until soft. Add mushrooms and cook for a moment. Remove from heat and mix through ham. Place this in the base of the case. Arrange the asparagus on top. Cut any firm stalks off and arrange like the spokes of a wheel. Mix eggs, cream, salt and pepper and pour over the top. Bake in moderate oven until set (about 20-25 minutes).
Serve hot or cold.

Asparagus Slice with Sesame Seed Topping

500 g (1 lb) asparagus
1 hard boiled egg
30 g (1 oz) soft butter
1 teaspoon mayonnaise
salt and pepper
125 g (¼ lb) puff pastry
1 beaten egg to glaze
1 tablespoon sesame seeds

Trim the asparagus and cook. Drain well and cut spears in halves if long. Mash the egg, add butter and mix well with mayonnaise, seasoning with salt and pepper.
Roll out the puff pastry very thinly. If it isn't really a thin casing, the dish is spoilt. Cut into 2 long strips, (about 23 x 15 cm or 9 x 6 inch). Spread one of the strips with the egg mixture. Arrange the asparagus pieces closely packed on top of this. Place the second piece on top and pinch the edges together. Brush top and edges with beaten egg. Then sprinkle lightly with the sesame seeds. Bake in a moderately hot oven, 190-200°C (375-400°F), about 12-15 minutes or until pastry is lightly browned.
Cut across into strips to serve. It is nicest served with a small jug of extra melted butter to pour over the top (if you don't mind a few extra calories!).

BEANS

French beans, string beans, green beans, whatever you may call them, they are a vegetable which can be served with almost any meat dish and if cooked in an interesting way can be used as a course on their own. Unfortunately it is not possible to buy the really small green beans that can be found in English and French markets. If you have your own vegetable garden you can pick them when very young and tiny and then cook them immediately. Otherwise you need to rely on buying them as fresh and young as possible. You can tell by the feel and the way they snap if they are fresh. Young beans don't need to have the strings removed, in fact most of the beans now sold are stringless and need only both ends removed. If they are larger pull the strings off first and then either cook whole or cut into large sections depending on your own preference.

BASIC METHOD OF COOKING: Beans lose colour, taste and texture if they are overcooked. The preliminary blanching can be done beforehand and then the beans used in various dishes and heated later. 500 g (1 lb) should serve 4 people, depending of course on the menu. Bring a pot of salted water to the boil, add the beans, cook slowly, uncovered until just tender but not soft. Drain as soon as tender and run cold water over them for a few minutes. This stops the cooking and instead of losing colour they remain green and have a better flavour. Leave to drain. Refrigerate (covered). Toss in butter to heat through before serving or use as required.

Almond Beans

500 g (1 lb) beans
60 g (2 oz) butter
1 bunch spring onions, chopped in small pieces
1 clove garlic, crushed
2 tablespoons slithered almonds
salt and pepper
2 teaspoons lemon juice

Top, tail and string the beans if necessary. Either leave whole or cut each bean into about 3 pieces. Cook them in a pan of salted water until just tender. Drain well. Melt the butter, add the spring onions, garlic and cook until the onions are tender. Add the almonds and cook until they are golden. Add beans, season with salt, pepper and lemon juice. The beans can be cooked beforehand and heated through again with the spring onion and almond mixture.

Spanish Beans

500 g (1 lb) beans
30 g (1 oz) butter
2 rashers bacon
2 garlic cloves, crushed
1 white onion, finely diced
2 ripe tomatoes, peeled, seeded, chopped small
1 cup chicken stock
1 tablespoon dry sherry
salt and pepper
½ teaspoon sugar

The best variety of beans for this dish are the stringless ones. If you have to string them, they tend to fall to pieces while they are cooking.
Trim the ends and cut them into short pieces. Melt the butter and cook the bacon, garlic and onion until softened. Add pieces of beans, tomatoes, stock, sherry, salt and pepper and sugar. Simmer covered until the beans are tender but not too soft. Remove the lid and boil away the liquid if there is too much. It should just be a nice thick sauce, enough to coat the beans.
This is a dish which is so flavoursome it is enough as a side dish on its own. Otherwise serve it with any plain cooked meat.

Savoury Beans

500 g (1 lb) green beans

Cook beans until just tender, leaving them whole. They could then be kept in a covered bowl in the refrigerator for as long as 24 hours before using.

30 g (1 oz) butter
1 rasher bacon
1 onion, finely sliced
1 tin tomatoes (about 450 g) drained, tomato chopped in half
2 cloves garlic, crushed
salt and pepper, 1 teaspoon sugar
4 tablespoons breadcrumbs
an additional 30 g (1 oz) melted butter

Melt butter, cook bacon and onion until soft, add tomato, garlic and seasoning. Cook uncovered 5 minutes until a thickish sauce. Place beans in a buttered shallow casserole and then add sauce. Top with breadcrumbs and lastly sprinkle over the melted butter. Can be kept 12 hours. Bake in moderate oven, 180-190°C (350-375°F), 20 to 25 minutes or until hot.

Broad Beans with Bacon

Broad beans are only nice if small and freshly picked; once they become large and strong, they are really best left in the shops.

500 g (1 lb) broad beans
30 g (1 oz) butter
1 clove garlic, crushed
1 white onion, finely chopped
3 rashers bacon, cut in small pieces
2 tablespoons cream
salt and pepper
1 tablespoon finely chopped parsley

Shell the broad beans and cook in salted water until tender. Melt the butter, add garlic, onion and bacon. Sauté until onion is tender and bacon crisp. Drain the beans and add. Pour in cream, season with salt and pepper. Warm and serve with the parsley mixed through at the finish.

PEAS

The French have always been outspoken in their admiration of peas and during the reign of Louis XIV, they were particularly well loved. During this reign, it was quite proper for the ladies at Versailles to delicately lick the peas from their pods after they had been dipped in a sauce. Women who had dined with the King would often hide a dish of peas and sneak them back to their chambers.

While spring peas have a wonderfully uniform tenderness, taste and colour that combine to make them one of the most delicate and popular vegetables, they were also the first ever vegetable to be tinned in the world, but peas that have been picked too large or kept too long usually resemble small hard green bullets.

Purée of Peas

This can be served with lamb dishes or can be mixed with noodles or pasta and served as a side dish with meat. The quantity makes enough to mix with 250 g (½ lb) cooked noodles.

60 g (2 oz) butter
1 white onion, finely diced
½ lettuce, cut up roughly
2 tablespoons chopped parsley
500 g (1 lb) fresh peas
1 teaspoon sugar
1 cup chicken stock
½ cup cream
½ cup finely diced ham

Melt the butter, sauté the onion, lettuce and parsley until softened. Add the peas, sugar, stock and cook, covered, until the peas are tender. Remove and put the juice and peas through a *moulin* or blend it. Return to the heat, add the cream and cook gently until it has thickened up and reduced slightly. Check for seasoning. Add the ham, warm through and serve. It has a delicate pale green colour and lovely flavour. When making this be careful that the stock is not too salty as the sauce will be reduced and this means it should be a little unsalted in the beginning.
If using with noodles, drain them well, mix in a little butter and then stir through the warm sauce.

Pea Soufflé

500 g (1 lb) fresh peas
30 g (1 oz) butter
1 white onion, finely diced
½ lettuce, broken into pieces
1 tablespoon finely chopped parsley
1 cup water
2 teaspoons sugar
1 teaspoon salt

Shell the peas. Melt butter and add onion, lettuce and parsley. Cook until slightly softened. Add water, peas, sugar and salt. Cover and cook until tender. Drain, put through *moulin* or blend. It should measure approximately 1 cup of purée.

30 g (1 oz) butter
1 tablespoon flour
¼ cup milk
the 1 cup pea purée
2 egg yolks
3 egg whites

Melt butter and add flour. Cook until foaming. Add milk and pea purée and cook until thick. Check at this stage for seasoning as it may need a little extra salt or pepper. Remove and leave to cool a few minutes. Add egg yolks. At the last minute beat the whites until very stiff and add ⅓ to mixture. Then fold remainder through gently. Pour into a 4 cup-size soufflé dish or casserole and bake for 25-30 minutes in a moderate oven 180-190°C (350-375°F). If you want it to rise up above the edge of the dish, tie a band of foil around the edge and use a slightly smaller dish.

Chinese Snow Peas

These are a special variety of peas whose pods have no parchment lining. They are nicest if picked when the peas inside the pods are still very small. Unfortunately, they are still not obtained easily in most shops but can always be bought during their season from Chinese shops or some stores which feature a large and selective greengrocery section. It is a pity because for the time they are in season, they give an excellent and fresh tasting change from the more usual green vegetables.

BASIC PREPARATION: Cut the tip and tail off, using scissors and if not so young, remove the stringy spine. Either cook whole or cut in half.

To Cook
1 tablespoon oil
500 g (1 lb) snow peas
salt and pepper
½ teaspoon sugar

Heat oil in a large pot. Add the peas, season with salt, pepper and sugar. Cover and cook for only a few minutes until they are tender but still crisp. Check for seasoning and serve.

Chinese Snow Pea Salad

250 g (½ lb) snow peas
125 g (¼ lb) bean shoots
1 tablespoon oil
4 medium sized button mushrooms, stalks removed
1 bunch spring onions

Cut tip and tail off snow peas. Leave whole. Wash the bean shoots and peas and drain well. Heat the oil in a large saucepan. Add the peas, cover, and cook 2 minutes. Add the bean shoots and cook over fairly high heat, stirring until they are tender but still crisp. Remove and leave to cool. Slice the mushrooms and the spring onions thinly. Mix with the dressing. Add the cooled peas and bean shoots and stand 30 minutes before serving.

Dressing
6 tablespoons peanut oil
2 tablespoons white wine vinegar
1 teaspoon sugar
salt and pepper
½ teaspoon dry English-style mustard.

Mix above ingredients together.

SOME OTHER SPRING VEGETABLES

Artichokes

Globe artichokes or leaf artichokes are a part of the thistle family and there are a great many varieties. These grow wild in areas of Europe but are now cultivated extensively. The edible parts are the base of the surrounding flower scales and the core of the 'choke'. They are eaten plainly boiled, leaf by leaf, with either melted butter, hollandaise sauce or vinaigrette.

When buying select young ones with close scales. The hearts are used a great deal in French cooking as a garnish with meat dishes and also served stuffed as a separate dish or accompanied by a sauce. They have a unique and delicate flavour and as they are quite expensive to buy here, it seems a shame to disguise this flavour by cooking them in elaborate or very rich ways.

BASIC METHOD OF COOKING: Trim off the stem of the artichoke and cut off about 2 cm (¾ inch) from the top end of the artichoke. Remove about 2 or 3 layers of the outer leaves. Rub the cut part with lemon to prevent darkening. Tie a thread around the widest part of the head. Put them into a saucepan of fast boiling water to which you have added salt and lemon juice. This helps to preserve the colour. Cook rapily until tender. This can take from 20-25 minutes depending on the size. Check by putting a fork into the base of one of the artichokes. If the fork meets no resistance and one leaf pulls away easily, the artichokes are cooked. Remove and drain. If necessary, squeeze gently to remove the excess water. Serve hot with melted butter or cold with vinaigrette sauce.

To Eat These: Pull off the leaves and dip the base into the butter or sauce. Scrape the base of the leaf between your teeth to remove the edible part and discard the remainder. When the leaves have been eaten, cut out the fuzzy 'choke' and discard it. The remaining part is then eaten with a fork. It is usual to serve 1 per person.

NOTE: This is an extremely frustrating thing to eat if you are really hungry; it has a lovely delicate flavour, but is purely meant to whet the appetite rather than satisfy it.

Stuffed Artichokes

Trim off the stem and points of the leaves. Plunge them into salted boiling water to which you have added the juice of 1 lemon for about 10 minutes. Drain and cool. Spread the leaves apart gently and using a spoon remove some of the centre and the furry looking choke, leaving a cavity for stuffing.

Stuffing:
1 cup breadcrumbs, made from stale bread
¼ cup milk
1 teaspoon finely chopped capers
1 small clove crushed garlic
2 tablespoons finely chopped parsley
1 tablespoon finely chopped anchovy fillets
250 g (½ lb) prawns, shelled, deveined and chopped

Place the breadcrumbs in a bowl and add the milk. Mix well, add capers, garlic, parsley, anchovy and prawns. Season with pepper. You probably won't need salt in this because the anchovy usually adds enough. Stuff the artichokes.

2 tablespoons oil
½ cup white wine

Place the above oil and white wine in a small casserole and place artichokes in this. Cover with a buttered piece of foil and cook in a moderate oven, 180-190°C (350-375°F), for about 30 minutes, basting occasionally until they are tender. Test with a fork.
Serve with a jug of melted butter. Eat the leaves first with butter and then eat the stuffing with the heart.

Beetroot

They are mostly associated with salads — standing fare in every country café, sitting astride a little mound of shaggy looking shredded lettuce — but deserve to be used in more interesting ways. Hot they are delicious and delicate and make a complete change as a vegetable.

BASIC METHOD OF COOKING: They must not be cut before cooking or they bleed, leaving them a little pale and anaemic looking. Cook whole in salted water and when tender leave to cool slightly. The skin will then slip off like removing a glove. They can also be put whole into the oven and baked the same as a potato. This gives them a good flavour but seems to take all day and is only worth while if you have the oven on for prolonged cooking.

Hot Beetroot Lyonnaise

This is only successful when made with small young beetroot.

6 beetroot
30 g (1 oz) butter
1 large white onion, finely chopped
salt and pepper
½ teaspoon sugar
2 teaspoons lemon juice
1 tablespoon cream

Place the beetroot in a pan of salted water, cover and cook until quite tender. Drain and leave to cool slightly. Slip off the skins, roots and stems. Melt the butter, add the onion and sauté until tender. Season with salt and pepper. Cut each beetroot into about 8 wedges. Add to the onion with sugar and lemon juice. Warm through. Lastly add cream and shake gently.
This is an interesting vegetable dish served with steaks or veal.

Baked Zucchini Mould

500 g (1 lb) small zucchini
little salt and pepper
60 g (2 oz) butter, cut in small pieces
1 small clove crushed garlic

Cut the top and base from the zucchini and cut into slices. Place in a saucepan and sprinkle with salt and pepper. Add butter and garlic. Place on a lid and cook in the butter until tender. Don't add any liquid. Shake the pan occasionally. Leave aside to cool.

2 eggs and 1 yolk
1 cup cream
¾ cup grated tasty cheese
little salt
pinch cayenne

Beat eggs, yolk, cream and cheese, adding salt and cayenne. Fold the cooled zucchini into this. Butter a 4 cup ovenproof dish and pour in mixture. Bake in a moderate oven, 180-190°C (350-375°F), standing the dish in a pan of water until just set (about 30 minutes but it depends on whether the dish is shallow or deep). This can be eaten warm or cold and is nice served with a tomato sauce made from cooked fresh tomatoes.

Zucchini with Tomato Topping

6 medium-sized zucchini

Cut in slices and cook until barely tender. Drain, put in shallow ovenproof dish.

60 g (2 oz) butter
2 tablespoons diced spring onions
pinch mixed herbs
salt and pepper
1 clove crushed garlic
3 thinly sliced tomatoes
* 3 tablespoons breadcrumbs, made from stale bread
2 tablespoons tasty cheese grated
60 g (2 oz) melted butter

Melt the butter and add the onion, herbs, salt, pepper and garlic. Mix this with the zucchini in the dish. It is best to do this while the zucchini is still warm as it seems to gain more flavour. Spread out in an even layer. Cover the top with the sliced tomatoes. Sprinkle these with salt and pepper, pinch sugar. Then spread the breadcrumbs and cheese over this. Lastly trickle the melted butter over and then bake in a moderate oven, 180-190°C (350-375°F), for about 25 minutes.

* *The quantity of breadcrumbs depends a bit on the size of the dish.*

NEW POTATOES

The first tiny new potatoes are so delicious that it hardly seems necessary to do anything but scrub them well and cook them with salt. Served with lashings of butter, nothing could be nicer. Because of their firm and waxy texture, they are best for salads, boiled in the skin and then peeled afterwards. Mixed with dressing while still warm it will soak in nicely. Unfortunately, a lot of small potatoes sold as new in the shops turn out to be anything but . . .

Potatoes in Mustard Sauce

1 kg (2 lb) new potatoes
1 tablespoon French mustard
1 tablespoon parsley, finely chopped
2 tablespoons cream
little extra salt and pepper

Scrub potatoes and cook in a pan of salted water. Drain well. Mix the mustard, parsley and cream together. When the potatoes are cooked pour this over the top and mix gently until potatoes are lightly coated.
Season with a little salt and pepper.

New Potatoes with Peppers

500 g (1 lb) tiny new potatoes
1 large red or green pepper
30 g (1 oz) butter
1 medium-sized white onion, finely diced
2 tablespoons finely chopped parsley
little salt and pepper

Scrub the potatoes and cook in salted water. Meantime, cut the pepper in half. Either hold over a gas flame until it is charred or put it under the griller for a few minutes. This may seem a bother but gives the dish a distinctive smokey flavour which is delicious. Pull the skin away, it will be like tissue paper and cut the pepper into strips.
Melt the butter and sauté onion until softened and golden. Add pepper strips, parsley and salt and pepper. It doesn't need cooking as the pepper strips will be already softened. Toss this gently with the drained potatoes. The pepper mixture can be made up beforehand and reheated gently just on dinner time.

Colombian Potatoes	**750 g (1½ lb) new potatoes, scrubbed**

Cook in salted water until tender. Drain well. Place in a casserole, cover with sauce and keep warm in the oven until serving time.

Sauce
30 g (1 oz) butter
1 white onion, finely chopped
2 ripe tomatoes, peeled, cut in small pieces
little salt and pepper
½ cup cream
½ cup tasty grated cheese
2 tablespoons finely chopped parsley

Melt butter and sauté onion until softened. Add tomatoes and season with salt and pepper. Cook about 10 minutes or until a thick sauce*. Add the cream and cheese and stir until the cheese melts. Add parsley last.
The first part up to * can be prepared in the morning but only add cream, cheese and parsley before serving.

SPRING LAMB

Spring ushers in a season of absolute delights, one of the prizes of which is spring lamb. In most European countries eating young lamb is associated only with spring, while butchers in Australia advertise it all year round. However, more than six months old and the meat becomes firm and stronger in flavour. Until recently lamb rarely appeared on restaurant menus here, an incredible fact for a country which has lamb which is as delicious and sweet as anywhere in the world.

As a quick, easy stand-by more lamb chops have probably been eaten per family than any other cut of the meat, now however they are becoming more expensive so perhaps will be treated as something rather special. The first of the baby spring chops which come into the shops really deserve to be cooked with care. Preheat the griller to very hot and brush the chops with a little melted butter mixed with a few finely chopped, fresh herbs.
If you don't have fresh ones just brush with some butter. Season with a little black pepper and grill until brown on the outside, salting after they are cooked. Timing depends on their thickness and whether you like them pink inside or a little more well done. Elaborate sauces are out of place with lamb, the flavour of the crispy outside and the moist, juicy flesh being complete in itself.

Lamb should never be grey if it is to be served at it's best, near the bone it should always be slightly pink, but while many people will eat rare beef they have a slight aversion to rare lamb.

The best way to roast a baby spring leg of lamb (or any leg of lamb for that matter) is to put it directly on the shelf in the oven. Leave the lamb to stand at room temperature first for an hour or so, cut a few slashes in the leg down towards the bone and insert slithers of garlic in these. Place a baking tin under the meat on a lower shelf and leave the lamb to cook on the shelf above at a moderate temperature, 180-190°C (350-375°F). If it starts to spit too much after a time you can turn the oven down slightly. This way the air circulates around it and there is no need to turn or touch it during the cooking. It will have a delicious, moist flesh with a beautiful crispy skin. Salt the meat after cooking. Potatoes or pumpkin, etc, can be cooked in the tin beneath the meat. Enough of the fat falls on them to give a good, brown colour but be sure to put them in about the same time as the meat as they take a little longer than usual to cook. Timing is difficult to give owing to personal taste but allow:
15 mins per 500 g (per lb) for pink lamb
20 mins per 500 g (per lb) for little more well done
25 mins per 500 g (per lb) for well done

Asparagus Vinaigrette à la Crême (see p. 7)

Baby Rack of Lamb Cutlets with Devilled Sauce

Order the lamb cutlets joined in sets of 3.

The top is trimmed down slightly. Score the back with a sharp knife in a diamond pattern. Cut two slashes near the bone and stud each with a slither of garlic. Wrap a little bit of foil around the bone to prevent charring and then bake in a moderate oven, 180-190°C (350-375°F), on the oven rack with a tray underneath to catch the drips:

25 minutes for rare
30 minutes, just pink
35 minutes, rather more well done.

Remove foil to serve. Serve with Devilled Sauce.

Devilled Sauce
90 g (3 oz) butter
¼ cup white wine vinegar
2 teaspoons dried tarragon
2 tablespoons water
3 egg yolks

Melt 60 g (2 oz) butter, keep aside. Cook vinegar and tarragon until the liquid has gone. Add water and egg yolks to this and then cooled melted butter. Stir until thick and don't let it get too hot or it will turn to scrambled eggs. Lastly add remaining 30 g (1 oz) of butter, diced small. Stir.

Add to This Basic Sauce
2 teaspoons French mustard
2 tablespoons finely chopped parsley
1 tablespoon diced bread and butter cucumber.

Sauce can be made hours beforehand and is served cold but not chilled.
It makes enough to serve with 6 sets of lamb cutlets.

Lamb in Orange Sauce

1 leg of lamb, (ask the butcher to bone it completely)
salt and pepper
30 g (1 oz) butter
2 tablespoons orange juice
2 tablespoons orange marmalade
1 clove crushed garlic

Cut the lamb through the centre, leaving it attached on one side. Put a skewer through to hold it out in a flat piece, rather like a butterfly shape. Salt and pepper the meat. Cook the butter, orange juice, marmalade and garlic in a saucepan until just boiling. Brush the lamb all over with this marinade and leave at room temperature for about 6 hours. Place directly on the centre rack in a moderate oven, 180-190°C (350-375°F), with a tray underneath with a small amount of water in it to catch the juice. This helps to prevent the oven becoming too messy. The lamb will take less time than usual to cook because of the way it is flattened out. Usually 45 minutes to 1 hour is sufficient but this depends on whether you like it really well done or slightly pink in the centre.

To Serve: Remove skewers and cut across in this slices. Serve with spiced jelly, potatoes and one plainly cooked green vegetable.

Spiced Jelly for Lamb
2 tablespoons red currant jelly
rind and juice of 1 large orange
1 tablespoon finely chopped mint
1 tablespoon white vinegar

Warm the red currant jelly with the rind and juice of the orange. Add mint when hot and smooth. Remove from the heat and then add vinegar. Chill and leave for 12 hours for the flavours to mature.

Cherry Fruit Bowl (see p. 24)

Lamb in Ratatouille

1 leg lamb about 1.5 kg (3 lb)
a few slithers of garlic
salt
1 medium-sized egg-plant
3 tablespoons oil
2 white onions, thinly sliced
2 garlic cloves, chopped
1 green pepper, cut in strips
2 medium-sized zucchini, sliced thinly
1 tin tomatoes or 3 fresh ripe ones, peeled
a little salt
pepper
1 teaspoon sugar
2 tablespoons parsley

Using a sharp knife make a few incisions into the lamb near the bone. Push in the slithers of garlic. Salt the lamb. Bake in a moderate oven, 180-190°C (350-375°F), directly on the rack for 30 minutes. Place a tray underneath to catch the drips from the lamb. This gets rid of some of the excess fat from the meat which would otherwise make the finished dish too greasy.
Cut egg-plant into dice and salt. Stand for ½ hour and then drain.
Heat oil, add onions, garlic, pepper, zucchini and sauté a few minutes or until slightly softened. Add eggplant and cook for another 5 minutes. Add tomatoes, salt pepper and sugar. Place the lamb on top of this mixture and cover the pan. This can either be cooked on top of the stove or in the oven. Cook for about 1½ to 2 hours or until the meat is very tender. The vegetable mixture is sprinkled with parsley just before serving. This dish can be kept warm for some time without spoiling.
Serve the lamb cut in slices with a border of the vegetables.

Mushroom Stuffed Loin of Lamb

1 loin of lamb of about 9 chops. Get your butcher to leave the bone in and the chop bone remains uncut. Salt and pepper the meat and bake it in a moderate oven, 180-190°C (350-375°F), for about 35 minutes. Cook it with the fat side up. Leave aside to cool for easier handling.

Filling
60 g (2 oz) butter
250 g (½ lb) mushrooms, thinly sliced
salt and pepper
½ cup finely diced ham
4 tablespoons breadcrumbs, made from stale bread

Melt the butter and add the mushrooms, cook until slightly softened, seasoning with salt and pepper. Remove to a bowl, add the ham and breadcrumbs. Add 4 tablespoons of the sauce or enough to make a soft and slightly moist mixture. Leave this filling aside to cool.

Sauce
60 g (2 oz) butter
2 large white onions, very finely diced
1 tablespoon and 2 teaspoons plain flour
1 cup chicken stock
pinch nutmeg

Melt the butter, sauté onions until softened. Add plain flour and cook until foaming, then add chicken stock and nutmeg and cook until thickened, stirring continuously. Leave to simmer gently for about 5 minutes. Either sieve, put through a *moulin* or blend the sauce.

To Assemble: When the loin is cool enough to handle cut the meat out of the bone in one long piece and cut into slices. You should get about 10 to 12 pieces. Spread a thin layer of the filling on the bone, place 1 of the pieces of meat back in its place, spread this with filling, then press on to this another slice of meat, more filling, etc, until the loin is reshaped in its original form. This is quite easy as the filling is sticky and moist, although sometimes it overlaps a little from both ends of the bone, if this happens, just press it firmly together. Spoon the remainder of the sauce over the top of the meat and leave aside at room temperature ready for cooking. This part can be done several hours before serving. Place onto a lightly buttered dish and bake in moderate oven, 180-190°C (350-375°F), for about 30 minutes.

It is nicest served with small new potatoes and a salad. This is a very rich dish and is plenty for 4 people but not quite enough for 6 unless they have fairly small appetites.

Orange Stuffed Loin of Lamb

1 loin of lamb, boned out
(This needs just a little of the flap left on so it can be rolled over easily.)
60 g (2 oz) butter
1 large white onion, finely chopped
1 clove garlic, crushed
2 rashers bacon, chopped
2 cups breadcrumbs, made from stale bread
grated rind of 1 orange
little salt and pepper
1 large egg
2 tablespoons orange juice

Melt butter, add onion, garlic and bacon. Cook until bacon is slightly crisp and onion tender. Place in a large bowl and mix in breadcrumbs, orange rind, salt and pepper. Bind with the egg and orange juice. Spread along the loin. Tie up with string. Bake in a dish in a moderate oven, 180-190°C (350-375°F), 1 hour for slightly pink in the centre — 1¼ hours for a little more well done.
Serve with Orange and Mint Sauce.

Orange and Mint Sauce
2 teaspoons cornflour
1 tablespoon red currant jelly
rind and juice of 1 large orange
½ cup stock — use lamb or a light stock such as chicken
1 tablespoon finely chopped mint
1 tablespoon white vinegar
segments of 1 large orange

Place in a saucepan, cornflour mixed with the red currant jelly, rind and juice of the orange, stock, mint, white vinegar and cook until lightly thickened. Peel the orange and remove the segments so no membrane is left on them. Add to the pan at the last moment and warm slightly.
The sauce can be made beforehand up to adding the orange pieces.

NOTE: You can use the lamb bones to make a good stock. Cover with water, add a little salt, onion and parsley. Bring to the boil, remove scum and simmer covered for a couple of hours. Strain and keep refrigerated.

Lamb Marinated in Apricot Sauce

Marinade
1 cup dried apricots
1 teaspoon sugar
30 g (1 oz) butter
1 large white onion, finely chopped
2 tablespoons mild curry
⅓ cup white wine vinegar
salt

Place apricots in saucepan with sugar. Just cover with water and cook gently until softened. Drain but keep aside ½ cup of the liquid. Sieve or *moulin* apricots. Melt butter and sauté onion until softened. Add curry and fry a moment. Add to this the liquid from the apricots, white wine vinegar and the puréed apricots. Season with a little salt.

1 small leg of lamb or 12 leg chops

Cut the lamb into bite-sized pieces. Mix meat with marinade and leave at room temperature 12 hours or refrigerated 24 hours. Remove from sauce and thread on skewers. Preheat griller and grill meat until cooked. It doesn't take long as the marinade tenderises it.
Serve as a dinner with Cucumber Salad, a rice dish, and some Mango Chutney.
This is not very highly spiced; if you would like it hotter add a little more curry to the marinade.

BEEF

The largest percentage of butchers use yearling beef instead of the larger ox beef as it is more convenient for suburban housewives who nowadays are serving smaller families. The size suits most requirements while the bones are of a more manageable proportion.

The flavour of prime yearling beef can almost match that of ox beef and although it doesn't always have quite the same taste, this obviously depends on the quality.

During the depths of winter, cattle from outer areas are often used, transporting methods having improved tremendously so beef is usually in plentiful supply. There is only a small quantity of grain-fed beef; it is excellent but can be a little more expensive. Sometimes too for varying reasons, such as very cold weather, the muscles stiffen, resulting in meat which may not be quite so good.

In later spring the animal has a very good flavour; the meat is lightly marbled with fat, and hopefully the price is usually lowered slightly so it is a good time to start using fillet, rump and more expensive cuts in dishes, leaving the casserole and slightly cheaper beef cuts for the winter months.

Spiced Fillets

6 thick pieces fillet steak
2 tablespoons Worcestershire sauce
2 tablespoons soy sauce
1 tablespoon barbecue sauce
½ teaspoon dry mustard
a little salt and pepper
1 clove crushed garlic
small piece of fresh ginger, grated, about ½ teaspoon

Mix all the marinade ingredients together. Flatten out the steak and dip in the marinade. Put on a large plate, cover with remainder of marinade and leave to stand several hours.

To Cook
1 tablespoon oil
1 large ripe tomato, skinned and chopped in small pieces

Remove the steaks from the plate, don't pat dry but just drain lightly. Heat the oil and when very hot brown the steaks both sides quickly, turn down heat slightly until just done as you wish. Remove and keep warm.
To Make a Sauce: Add the pieces of tomato to the pan, a few spoons of marinade and let simmer about 1 minute. Serve on top of steak.

Delight of the Gourmet

6 thick pieces of fillet steak
60 g (2 oz) butter
2 tablespoons finely chopped parsley
1 clove crushed garlic
pinch salt, good pinch of cayenne pepper

Trim away all outside fat and sinew from each piece of fillet. With a sharp knife cut out the centre meat in one piece to make a small case and keep aside the centre piece. Mash together the butter, parsley, garlic, salt and cayenne until smooth. Put some of this butter in the centre hole and then replace the piece of meat. Press firmly together. If it looks uneven just form gently into a circle again. This is easy as the meat is quite pliable.

French mustard
plain flour, seasoned with a little salt and pepper
1 large egg beaten with 1 tablespoon oil
breadcrumbs

Spread a little French mustard on top of the meat. Dip each fillet slice first in flour, then egg and lastly breadcrumbs. Leave refrigerated for 1 hour for the butter to firm.

To Cook
2 tablespoons peanut or vegetable oil
2 tablespoons butter

Heat oil and butter together and when foaming and very hot cook the steaks on both sides. These have to be cooked a little slower than is usual for steak or else the breadcrumbs go too brown. I usually cook them 4-5 minutes both sides, but this time is a matter of personal taste as to whether you like them very rare or just pink and of course depends on the thickness of the steaks. During the cooking the butter gradually melts and soaks into the meat making this one of the juiciest and most flavoursome fillets imaginable. The dish can be prepared beforehand and left for 12 hours before cooking.

Steak Savini

This sauce can be used on either well trimmed pieces of fillet steak, or if you prefer rump steak can be served. Buy a tender steak; 500 g (1 lb) serves 2 to 3 depending on the rest of the dinner. If using rump cut small incisions around the edge of the fat so it will not curl up. Make sure the steak is dry; a moist steak will not brown successfully.

1 tablespoon Worcestershire sauce
1 teaspoon French mustard
1 clove crushed garlic
½ cup cream
30 g (1 oz) pâté de foie

Measure out above ingredients and place into a bowl. They don't need to be mixed as during the cooking of the sauce they will blend together.

To Cook
1 tablespoon oil
30 g (1 oz) butter

Heat in a large pan and when the foam is about to subside add the steaks and cook over fairly high heat 3 or 4 minutes on each side, although this timing is very much a matter of personal taste. Often the easiest way to tell if they are ready is to cut a tiny incision in one of the pieces of meat. Salt and pepper them after cooking and keep warm in the oven while preparing the sauce which only takes a couple of minutes to cook.
Tip the fat from the pan. Add the sauce ingredients and heat using a fork to mash and stir them together until a smooth sauce is formed.
Don't let it boil if possible, not because it curdles or separates, but rather because the pâté is delicate and only needs to be warmed through.
Serve a little on top of each steak.

Steak Townhouse

1 piece of rump steak in a thick piece-weight about 1.5 kg (3 lb)
a little oil
60 g (2 oz) butter
1 clove crushed garlic
1 tablespoon finely chopped parsley
a little Worcestershire sauce
salt and pepper

Rub the steak with a little oil on the outside. Slash the fat. Place in a baking tin in a hot oven, 200-220°C (400-425°F). It is difficult to give an exact time for this as it depends whether the steak is a fat thick piece, or a longer thinner piece. It can take between 25 to 45 minutes. It also depends of course on whether you like it rare or medium.
While the steak is cooking, mash the butter, garlic, and parsley together. Spread this ready waiting for the steak on a platter. Sprinkle the butter with a little Worcestershire sauce. When the steak is ready place it on top of the butter on the platter; pepper and salt it. Leave 30 seconds and then turn over. The butter will melt and coat the outside of the steak, giving it a delicious flavour. Cut the meat down in thin slices, slightly on the slant, serving a little of the juices with each portion.

Marinated Steak with Green Peppercorns

1 piece rump or grilling steak (about 1 to 1.5 kg or 2-3 lb)
¾ cup dry vermouth
1 large clove garlic, crushed
1 tablespoon green peppercorns, crushed slightly

Make small slashes through the fat on the side of the steak. Place in a china or plastic container and cover with the vermouth. Add garlic and peppercorns. Leave to marinate for about 5 hours. Remove and dry the steak with kitchen paper. Preheat the oven to moderately hot, 200-220°C (425-450°F). Cook until done to the degree you like. Exact timing is difficult to give because it depends whether the steak is a longer thinner piece or a small fat piece. It will cook fairly quickly owing to the marinade. Thin pieces — about 20 minutes should be enough; fat pieces — 30 minutes or so. Remove and salt lightly. While the steak is cooking, make the sauce.
Place the vermouth and peppercorn marinade in a small saucepan.

Add 3 tablespoons port and cook until it is reduced to about half. Add 1 tablespoon cream

Place the meat on a heated platter. Cut down to make small, thin slices. Spoon a little sauce over each serving. The sauce is rather liquid so don't mix it with vegetables on the same plate. Small potatoes and salad are best.

Mediterranean Stuffed Fillet

6 slices fillet steak

Trim well and flatten gently until a round circle. Season with salt and pepper.

Filling
60 g (2 oz) butter
2 medium-sized white onions, sliced very thinly
1 green pepper, cut in strips
1 clove garlic, crushed
1 large ripe tomato, peeled and cut in dice
pinch thyme
pinch rosemary
6 anchovy fillets, roughly chopped
2 tablespoons finely chopped parsley
pepper, (no salt as the anchovies are usually quite salty enough)
1 egg

Melt butter, add onion and pepper and cook until soft. Add garlic, tomato, thyme and rosemary and cook about 10 minutes or until a thick sauce. Add anchovy fillets, parsley, pepper and egg and cook a moment stirring until thickened. Remove and cool. Spread this on one side of fillet, fold over and use a couple of small wooden toothpicks to hold it together.

To Cook
1 tablespoon oil
15 g (½ oz) butter

Heat oil and butter, add steaks. Brown over high heat on both sides. Transfer to the oven and cook at a moderate heat, 180-190°C (350-375°F), for 8-12 minutes (depending on how well you like your meat done).

CHERRIES

Queen Victoria thought so highly of the cherry she had an orchard planted near Windsor to provide her with all the fresh cherries she desired. She had a passion for cherry tart and it was one of the dishes the eighteen year old queen requested at her coronation banquet. Elizabeth I was also very fond of the fruit and has been credited somewhat erroneously with the planting of the first cherry orchard. However, more than a century before this several kinds of wild cherries grew in profusion in Kent and other counties and London fruit vendors hawked 'cherries on the twig' to the cry of 'cherry ripe'.

There are almost 500 varieties now cultivated and it is the commonest garden fruit in temperate climates. Mostly they fall into three categories, sweet cherries of which the red bing is the leading variety, sour cherries, the pale amarelles and red and black morello and duke cherries, neither sweet nor sour but a hybrid of the two.

Cherry Fruit Bowl

500 g (1 lb) cherries
¼ cup water
good pinch cinnamon
grated rind of 1 orange
3 tablespoons sugar
¼ cup claret
juice of 1 orange
1 tablespoon brandy
2 tablespoons red currant jelly
1 punnet strawberries

Place cherries, water, cinnamon, grated rind of orange and sugar in a saucepan.
Heat until the juices run; add the claret. Cook gently until cherries are just tender.
Add orange juice and brandy and mix in red currant jelly. Stir over low heat until the jelly is dissolved.
Cool and then chill. Several hours before serving add strawberries. The cherry mixture keeps well for 4 to 5 days.

Cherry Mould

Serves 8

1 tablespoon and 1 teaspoon gelatine
¼ cup water
2 cups claret
rind of 1 lemon
2 tablespoons lemon juice
¾ cup sugar
few drops vanilla essence
250 g (½ lb) cherries
1 tablespoon brandy
½ cup red currant jelly

Mix gelatine and water together and stir. Dissolve standing over hot water. Heat the claret with lemon rind, lemon juice, sugar and vanilla. Add the cherries, cover and cook them until tender. Remove the cherries with a spoon. Cool slightly. The dessert is nicer if the stones are now removed from the cherries. (This is a bit tedious but worth the trouble.) Add the brandy and red currant jelly to the claret and stir until the red currant jelly is dissolved. Heat again if necessary. Add gelatine, cherries and then cool. Pour into a 6 cup mould. Chill until set.

Lemon Yoghurt Base
1 tablespoon gelatine
2 tablespoons water
¾ cup castor sugar
rind of 1 lemon
¼ cup lemon juice
1 cup plain yoghurt
¾ cup cream

Mix gelatine and water together and stir. Dissolve standing over hot water. Place sugar, lemon rind and juice in a basin and stir. Add gelatine and mix well. Stir in yoghurt. Beat cream until stiff and fold through last. Pour this on to the set cherry jelly. Chill. This sets very quickly. Turn out by dipping the mould in a little warm water.

Cherry Soufflé Custard

This is a soufflé-type dish with one difference — it doesn't collapse when taken out of the oven and can be served hot, warm or cold.

6 egg yolks
½ cup sugar
60 g (2 oz) butter
2 teaspoons grated lemon rind
¼ cup lemon juice

Place all above ingredients in a basin or double boiler. Cook over simmering water until thick and smooth, stirring occasionally. Do not let it get too hot. When thickened, cool, stirring occasionally.

Cherry Mixture
250 g (½ lb) cherries
1 tablespoon sugar

Place cherries in a saucepan with sugar. Cover and cook over a low heat until just barely softened. Leave to cool and remove stones. This is essential as apart from the fact it's easy to crack a tooth on them, the weight of the stones means the cherry sinks to the base of the dish.
Fold the cherries into the lemon custard.

Beat until stiff 6 egg whites
Add 2 tablespoons castor sugar

Beat again until very stiff.
Fold through the mixture gently.
Spoon into ungreased 4 cup casserole or baking dish. Set this dish in a pan of water to come half way up. Bake in oven, 160-180°C (325-350°F), for about 35 minutes or until a knife inserted 5 cm (2 inch) from the edge comes out clean.
Serve with a jug of cream.
The lemon mixture can be prepared beforehand and the cherries added, but leave the egg whites until close to cooking time for the best result.

Frosted Cherries

Serves 10

These are simple to do, will keep for a couple of days, except in very humid weather and look beautiful for a party. They are especially good if you have a sweet tooth.

500 g (1 lb) dark ripe cherries
1 large egg white (or sometimes you may even need 2)
castor sugar

Leave the stalks on the cherries. Wash and put aside to dry. Beat the egg white with a fork for a couple of seconds until just slightly frothy, but don't make it stiff. Dip the cherries in the egg white using the stalks to handle them. Then hold for a moment to let the excess drain away. Roll around lightly to get rid of any loose castor sugar. Place these on a cake rack in a warm dry place in the kitchen until the sugar has formed a coating. This usually takes a couple of hours.

GOOSEBERRIES

The early gooseberries, the small green and rather hard ones make the best pies, jams and desserts. Later when they become fatter and sweeter they are not at their best from the cooks point of view. Perhaps many people are not keen to try them because of the work involved in preparing them and the pippy taste. However the following recipes use them in a purée form, giving the flavour without pips and there is no need to top and tail them before cooking.

One of the earliest gooseberry preparations was a sauce served with mackerel, this gave the fruit its French name *Groseille a maquerear*, and this same sauce is also delicious with pork, veal, lamb, goose or duck.

Nowadays the fruit is not so widely grown in France and certainly not very widely grown here, but for a few short weeks in spring, boxes appear in the shops and this sweet-sour flavour is well worth trying.

Gooseberry Sauce

For this, use the early tart green gooseberries. It is an excellent sauce to serve with pork, roasted veal or duck.

500 g (1 lb) gooseberries
¼ cup water
30 g (1 oz) butter
2 tablespoons sugar
pinch salt
pinch nutmeg

Because the gooseberries are going to be sieved, just wash. It is not necessary to top and tail them. Place in a saucepan with the water, cover and cook until tender. Put through a sieve or *moulin*. While hot, mix in butter, sugar, salt and nutmeg. The sauce can either be served hot or cold and can be made well beforehand and reheated. Sometimes the sugar may need adjusting; it depends on the tartness of the gooseberries.

Gooseberry Meringue Tart

This is much more interesting than a lemon meringue tart. It has a sharp refreshing and yet rather elusive flavour, with a very melt-in-the-mouth soft crust. Despite the fact that it has a crust, filling and meringue and appears a heavy sweet, it is very light in reality and so can be served successfully even after a quite substantial main course.

Champagne Pastry
60 g (2 oz) butter
2 tablespoons sugar
1 egg yolk
1 cup S.R. flour
2 tablespoons cornflour
2 tablespoons sugar

Cream together the butter and sugar. When fluffy, add the egg yolk. Sift in the dry ingredients and mix to a dough. Knead lightly. Roll out and fit into flan tin 23 cm-25 cm (9-10 inch). Press down gently and bake in a moderate oven, 180-190°C (350-375°F), until a pale golden brown (about 15-20 minutes).

Filling
250 g (½ lb) gooseberries
¼ cup water

Place berries and water in a saucepan (it isn't necessary to top and tail them). Cover and cook over low heat until they are softened. Then put through a sieve or *moulin*. It should measure about ½ cup of pulp.

30 g (1 oz) butter
½ cup sugar (this depends on the sweetness of the pulp; you may not need quite this much)
1 tablespoon plain flour
2 eggs, separated

Cream the butter and sugar together until fluffy. Add the plain flour and egg yolks. Fold in the gooseberry pulp and pour into tart case. Bake in moderate oven, about 15 minutes or until it is set, at 180-190°C (350-375°F) and firm to touch. Leave to cool for a few minutes.

Meringue
2 egg whites
2 tablespoons castor sugar
½ teaspoon vanilla essence

Beat the egg whites until very stiff, add the sugar and vanilla and beat again until a stiff meringue. Spread over gooseberry filling. Return to hot oven, 200-220°C (400-425°F), and bake about 5-6 minutes or until tinged with gold.

Gooseberry Cream

The filling from the tart can be used as a dessert on its own. Cook it either in a large ovenproof dish, or else in small individual soufflé or similar type casseroles. Make up the gooseberry filling as for the pie. Double it using 500 g (1 lb) gooseberries as the smaller quantity on its own does not make enough for 6.
Butter the dish or dishes well, pour in the gooseberry filling and bake. A large dish will take about 25 minutes, small dishes about 15 minutes in a moderate oven, 180-190°C (350-375°F). When it is just set, cover the top with the meringue and bake again until meringue is just tinged with gold. The dessert can be served hot, warm or cold.

HERBS AND SPICES

The use of herbs in cooking is one of the easiest ways to bring some adventure into the kitchen. While each has a special place, some have more of an affinity with one food than another.

Mostly the only ones possible to buy in the shops are the familiar mint and parsley, so it is necessary to have a small garden plot, window box or a few small pots to have a supply of fresh ones on hand.

While some fresh herbs flourish throughout the year, they start to really gain their new growth as the weather warms, and many are annuals, useable fresh from later in spring through to summer. At other times of the year it is necessary to use them dried, remembering they are often stronger in flavour. They should be bought in small quantities and used quickly or a certain mustiness can sometimes be detected.

Besides their value in flavouring food, herbs have traditionally been used in the preparation of medicines, and Hippocrates, the 'Father of Medicine', left a list of four hundred simple herbs used medicinally, half of which are still in use today.

Whether we take them, eat them, or grow them, herbs and spices play an important part in cooking and are an important part of history. Legends and stories about their value have been handed down through the ages.

There are several excellent books published purely on the subject of herbs in cooking. It would be impossible in this one section to more than just touch on their uses, yet it would be remiss not to mention them as a part of the springtime scene.

Basil

A symbol of love in Italy, it is a sacred herb in India and a belief is held that a house surrounded by basil bushes is well blessed. This comes in a variety of types but the best two are sweet basil and bush basil. It is known best for its particular affiliation with tomatoes, on salads, over halved tomatoes before grilling or in sauces. A little basil used when cooking oily fish cuts down on the rich taste.

Stuffed Ham Rolls with Basil

Filling
30 g (1 oz) butter
1 large white onion, finely diced
1 large ripe tomato, skinned and chopped small
1 teaspoon chopped fresh basil
salt and pepper
1 teaspoon sugar
2 large hard boiled eggs
½ teaspoon dry, English-style mustard
2 tablespoons breadcrumbs (made from stale bread)
1 tablespoon finely chopped parsley
6 thin slices ham

Melt the butter and sauté onion until golden, add tomato, basil, salt, pepper and sugar and cook rapidly until thick. Place into bowl. Mash eggs, mix with mustard, breadcrumbs and parsley and stir into tomato mixture. It will be quite moist. Spread some of this filling on each slice of ham. Roll over and press firmly to hold in a long roll. Chill a few minutes.

Coating
plain flour, seasoned with a little salt and pepper
1 large egg, beaten with 1 tablespoon oil
breadcrumbs.

Dip each roll in flour, then egg and finally breadcrumbs. Keep refrigerated until ready to cook. They can be prepared beforehand and kept for about 12 hours without spoiling.

To Cook
2 tablespoons oil
30 g (1 oz) butter

Heat oil and butter until foaming. Add ham rolls and cook turning once until heated through and golden on all sides.
Serve with a little mustard and mayonnaise.

To Make This Mix
2 teaspoons hot, English-style mustard
2 tablespoons cream
1 teaspoon mayonnaise

This makes an interesting entrée or lunch dish. Serve 2 per person for lunch though.

Chives

This is the most delicate of the onion family and has many uses with eggs, cheese, new potatoes, salads, soups and is especially good if used in conjunction with parsley.

Scallops in Chive Butter

500 g (1 lb) scallops
60 g (2 oz) butter
1 small clove garlic crushed
2 tablespoons finely chopped parsley
2 tablespoons finely chopped chives
2 teaspoons lemon juice
black pepper

Remove the coral from the scallops. Cut the scallops into slices. Chop the coral small and mix together. Place into six small ovenproof dishes and sprinkle the top with a little salt and pepper.
Mash the butter until soft, mix with garlic, parsley chives, lemon and black pepper. Spread, or dot this over the top of the scallops.
Place in a moderate oven, 180-190°C (350-375°F), for about 10 minutes or until scallops are cooked. Be careful not to spoil them by overcooking. The sauce which forms is delicious and you need to serve some nice crusty bread to mop it up.

Dill

This grows easily, almost like a weed and is an annual. The name stems from the Norse word 'dilla' which means to lull. Dill water, a concoction made from the seeds was given to small babies to soothe them in Saxon times, just as it is often used still today.
It is good sprinkled over bread or rolls, with fish or vegetables in pickles, potato dishes or sauerkraut.

Potatoes cooked with Dill

This potato dish goes very well with fish, veal or pork.

1 kg (2 lb) potatoes
1 cup milk
1 cup cream
1 teaspoon salt
little pepper
1 teaspoon chopped dill

Peel potatoes, if large cut in halves or quarters. Place in a saucepan with milk, cream, salt, pepper and dill. Cook with the lid off until tender. This usually takes about 35 to 45 minutes and the liquid will thicken up and become almost like a sauce.

VARIATION: Prepare potatoes as above and before serving cook 1 large diced white onion in 45 g (1½ oz) butter until softened. Scatter this over the potatoes.

Parsley

It must always be very fresh and can be used lavishly both for flavouring and garnishing. Remember that for cooking the stalks have more flavour than the leaves.

Parsley Butter

This can be used with steak or spread on toast as a savoury. It is also good in a breakstick. Cut 1 long fresh breadstick down in slices, spread between each slice with the parsley butter and bake about 10 minutes in the oven. It has a lot more flavour and colour than garlic bread.

60 g (2 oz) butter
1 clove garlic, crushed
3 tablespoons finely chopped parsley
1 tablespoon grated tasty cheese
little pepper
1 teaspoon French mustard
pinch dry, English-style mustard.

Mash all ingredients together.
This makes enough for 1 breadstick, but can easily be doubled if you wish.

Rosemary

There are probably more legends around this herb than any other. It was always supposed to ward off bad magic and sprigs of rosemary to this day symbolize friendship and remembrance.

   With its spicy scent it goes best with lamb or mutton. The leaves are rather thin and spiky so it is essential to cut them up very finely so your guest won't get mouthfuls of them.

Rosemary Butter

Use on lamb chops before grilling.

60 g (2 oz) butter
1 tablespoon olive oil
1 clove crushed garlic
black pepper
1 teaspoon lemon juice
1 sprig rosemary, cut very finely

Place above ingredients in a saucepan and heat. Leave to cool slightly and use, brushing on the chops before grilling. If you can't spare the time to cut the rosemary finely, crush or bruise the sprig lightly, heat and then remove before using the butter.
Enough butter for about 12 small chops.

Sage

Sage is a rather strong and pungent herb. It is best in stuffings for goose, veal or pork but be careful to only use a little.

Meat Balls with Sage

500 g (1 lb) beef, finely minced
250 g (½ lb) pork, finely minced
1 large egg
½ cup breadcrumbs, made from stale bread
½ teaspoon brown sugar
1 teaspoon salt
1 teaspoon finely chopped fresh sage
1 medium-sized potato
½ cup milk

Mix in a large basin the beef, pork, egg, breadcrumbs, brown sugar, salt, sage. Peel potato and cook in salted water until tender. Drain well and mash. Add the milk and beat until fluffy. Fold this into the meat mixture. It will be very easy to handle. Roll into small balls and dust these with a little plain flour.

To Cook
a little oil to cover the base of a frying pan
a small piece of butter
1 cup cream
salt and pepper

Heat the oil and butter and when very hot add the meatballs a few at a time. Cook, shaking the pan occasionally so they roll over and are lightly browned on the outside. Transfer to a casserole as they cook and continue until they are all ready. Cover with cream, season with a little salt and pepper. (Instead of covering with cream, you may put a cup of any light sauce, such as mushroom, tomato, etc. over the top). Cover the casserole and bake about 20 minutes in a moderate oven 180-190°C (350-375°F).
Makes about 40 small meat balls.

Tarragon

French tarragon has a much better flavour than any other in cooking but it can only be grown from cuttings or root divisions and these are sometimes difficult to get. It adds flavour to chicken and is traditional as a garnish for cold eggs in jelly, in cold sauces and is an important ingredient in many of the great classic sauces of France.

Chicken Livers in Wine and Tarragon Sauce

Instead of chicken livers, this dish can also be made using kidneys.

500 g (1 lb) chicken livers, cut in halves
60 g (2 oz) butter
1 clove garlic, crushed
2 rashers bacon, diced small
2 teaspoons plain flour
1 ripe tomato, peeled and diced
2 teaspoons chopped tarragon
1 cup white wine
salt and pepper
¼ teaspoon sugar
¼ cup cream

Wash the livers and dry them. Melt butter, add garlic and bacon and cook a couple of minutes. Add livers and turn until they have changed colour. Add flour and stir until the flour is lightly coloured. Add tarragon, tomato, white wine, salt and pepper and sugar. Cook gently, stirring until it is lightly thickened. Simmer a few minutes, adding cream at the finish.
This dish can be made beforehand and then reheated gently.
Serve with rice or just crusty bread as the sauce is too nice to leave.

Green Peppercorn

The most popular spice in the world is the pepper, black or white, but recently a comparatively new product, the small green peppercorn has appeared to stir interest. It took the Malagasy Republic to devise a method of canning it to make it available for consumption and this has stimulated the development of many new recipes and additions to classical ones. Peppercorns which grow in clusters are picked before reaching full maturity. After exposure to the sun they become dark and hard; the white ones are just the black peppercorns with the outer hulls removed.

But the green peppercorns are picked fresh and tinned while soft and green so they have a pungent and very fresh taste. They come in brine or water and after opening, any unused berries should be kept refrigerated, or else kept frozen in small ice cream cubes. They can be used whole, mashed or chopped.

Green Peppercorn Butter

60 g (2 oz) butter
1 tablespoon green drained peppercorns, mashed
1 tablespoon finely chopped parsley
1 small clove garlic, crushed

Mash the butter well, add the peppercorns, parsley, garlic and mix well. Leave to stand at room temperature for a short time for the flavours to blend and then chill until firm. Form into small balls about the size of walnuts, flatten. Keep chilled.
This butter can be served with steak, lamb or put on top of large potatoes baked in their skins.

Paprika

Paprika is one of the most widely used of all the ground capsicum peppers, giving both a distinctive colour and piquancy to dishes. Made from the dried fruits of any of several sweet varieties of peppers, its flavour depends on the type and part selected. The most concentrated source of hotness is in the seeds. The purest paprika consists only of the walls of the pepper pod, the lowest from the seed. Most qualities come somewhere between these two extremes. As a rule Spanish is milder than Hungarian. Although the Hungarian paprikas are the finest, even the pods are carefully graded.

Paprika has a variety of uses in cooking although unfortunately is often thought of as merely something pretty to sprinkle on top of food.

Paprika Rice Stuffing

This is excellent in chicken. It makes sufficient to stuff 1 large chicken about 1.75 kg (approximately 3¼ lb)

1 small pork chop
60 g (2 oz) butter
1 white onion, finely diced
1 tablespoon paprika
¾ cup cooked long grain rice
1 clove crushed garlic
4 chopped pimento stuffed olives
3 tablespoons breadcrumbs
1 small ripe tomato, peeled and diced
1 egg
salt and pepper

Remove the fat from the pork chop and dice the pork up very small. Melt the butter, add onion and pork and cook until the meat is tender. Add paprika and cook over gentle heat for a minute. Place the rice, garlic, olives, breadcrumbs, tomato and egg in a bowl. Add the onion and pork mixture and stir well, seasoning with pepper and salt.

Summer

ICED SOUPS

Chilled soups have a refreshing quality which makes them ideal on warm summer evenings. Quite often a slight look of shock comes across the face of a guest at the first mouthful, purely as the majority of people still think of soup mostly as a hot course. Should the weather change drastically and suddenly, it is possible to warm most iced soups and use them instead as piping hot starters.

Among these recipes neither Paradise Soup nor the Chodlick are successful as hot soups, so if the weather does change you will just have to grin and turn up the heating.

Be especially careful when using stock in iced soups that it is completely free of any fat or this will ruin the soup.

Snow Soup

2 white onions
1 large Granny Smith apple
2 stalks celery
2 medium-sized potatoes
4 cups chicken stock
1 teaspoon sugar
1 teaspoon curry powder
1 teaspoon salt
1 cup cream
chives to garnish

Chop all vegetables quite finely. Place in a pot with stock and seasonings. Cook until very tender and blend or put through *moulin* sieve until a smooth mixture. Chill. Add cream to the soup and check for seasonings. Serve with a few chopped chives on top.

Artichoke and Pea Soup

2 leeks
½ lettuce
30 g (1 oz) butter
2 tablespoons dried peas
1 tin artichokes (about 240 g or 7½ oz) drained well
4 cups chicken stock
1 cup cream

Chop the leeks into thin slices. If leeks are unobtainable, use 1 large white onion, finely chopped instead. Break the lettuce up into pieces. Melt butter and sauté leeks and lettuce until softened. Add peas, artichokes chopped roughly and chicken stock. Simmer, covered, until the vegetables are softened. Put soup through *moulin* or sieve or blend until quite smooth. Check for seasoning. Chill. Before serving, add the cream and stir well. It keeps well for about 2 days. If it is a little too thick, thin with extra chicken stock.

Paradise Soup

750 g (1½ lb) ripe tomatoes
2 teaspoons sugar
1 teaspoon salt
1 teaspoon grated onion
juice ½ lemon
1 teaspoon lemon rind
3 cups chicken stock (chicken cubes can be used for this)
2 tablespoons cream

Garnish
2 slices ham
1 small cucumber
a little finely chopped parsley or chives

Chop tomatoes roughly and push through a *moulin* or sieve. It isn't necessary to skin them as the *moulin* will keep the skin from going through. If you prefer to use a blender, skin the tomatoes first and remove the seeds.
Add sugar, salt, onion, lemon and stock to tomato pulp. Chill well.
At serving time add cream and mix.
Garnish: Cut ham in strips. Skin cucumber, cut away the firm part in long strips and dice. Salt. Stand 1 hour and drain. Mix ham and cucumber into soup. Top with parsley or chives. Must be served really cold.

Chilled Chodlick

2 medium-sized beetroot or 3 tiny ones
4 cups chicken stock
1 teaspoon sugar
3 tablespoons lemon juice
salt and pepper
1 cucumber
2 hard boiled eggs, finely chopped
6 spring onions, diced finely
125 g (4 oz) prawns, shelled and deveined
½ cup cream

Grate the beetroot; cook in the stock with sugar for about 5 minutes. Strain. Season the liquid with the lemon juice and salt and pepper, if needed. Chill. Grate cucumber; add a little salt and stand 1 hour. Drain and press out excess liquid. Mix the cucumber with eggs and spring onions. Chop prawns finely and add.
To Serve: Mix soup with cucumber mixture and lastly stir in the cream. It should be a bright clear red colour and must be served icy cold. The base can be kept for 2 days but once you have added the cucumber, egg etc., it must be used within 6 hours. The beetroot which was used to colour the soup will be fairly tender and can still be used, although it will be a paler colour than usual. Mixed with oil and vinegar, a little seasoning of salt, pepper and sugar, it makes a good side salad the next day. Or you can add finely diced white onion and a little sour cream to it as an alternative.

SUMMER APPETIZERS

The first course in a summer menu should be light, interesting and fresh in colour and taste. As a rule appetites are smaller and so the purpose of these dishes is to stimulate, rather than saturate.

Eggs in Caviar Sauce

1 large ripe tomato
1 tablespoon mayonnaise
2 tablespoons lightly whipped cream
2 teaspoons lemon juice
¼ teaspoon tabasco
little salt and pepper
1 jar black caviar, about 45 g (1½ oz). (It is not necessary to use Russian caviar in a dish like this, the price is too high for it to be mixed in a sauce.)
6 hard boiled eggs

Cut the tomato into pieces and put through a *moulin* or sieve. Add mayonnaise, cream, lemon, tabasco and season with salt and pepper. Add caviar only at the last moment as otherwise it will darken the sauce. It doesn't alter the flavour but it is not so attractive in appearance. Cut the eggs in halves and place cut side down on small plates. Spoon enough sauce over the top to coat each half. Serve with triangles of buttered bread or hot French bread.

Pineapple Cocktail

1 small pineapple
1 large grapefruit
2 tablespoons sugar
4 sprigs of mint
juice of 1 orange
1 tablespoon gin

Peel pineapple. Remove core and cut into pieces. Peel grapefruit and carefully remove segments leaving membrane behind. Place pineapple and grapefruit in a bowl with the sugar and leave to stand for several hours. Drain away juices and place it in a saucepan with mint and orange juice. Warm until boiling. Pour hot over fruit and refrigerate for 12 hours. Remove the mint, add the gin and place in small dishes or champagne glasses with a fresh sprig of mint on top. This is a terrific pick-me-up for breakfast or else a refreshing dessert or appetizer for summer.

Egg Mousse with Spiced Sauce

2 teaspoons gelatine
2 tablespoons water
6 hard boiled eggs
4 tablespoons mayonnaise
3 teaspoons anchovy sauce
4 tablespoons cream
¼ teaspoon salt
white pepper
1 egg white

Mix gelatine and water together. Stir. Dissolve over hot water. Mash eggs; mix with mayonnaise, anchovy sauce, cream, salt and pepper. Add gelatine. Lastly beat egg white until stiff and fold through. Check for seasoning. This depends a lot on the flavour of the mayonnaise. Set in a small bowl (between 3 and 4 cups size). Turn out and serve with a Cucumber Salad and Spiced Sauce.

Spiced Sauce
1 tomato, peeled and diced
salt and pepper
1 teaspoon sugar
1 teaspoon curry
1 tablespoon Worcestershire sauce
1 tablespoon mayonnaise
1 large pimento (Spanish pimento can be bought in small tins.)
3 tablespoons oil
1 tablespoon white vinegar

Cook tomato slowly with pepper, salt, sugar until soft. Add curry. Remove from heat. Leave to cool then add remaining ingredients. Serve cold. This keeps for days. Remove from refrigerator about 1 hour before using as otherwise it is too thick.

Moulded Seafood Salad

2 medium-sized cooked potatoes, diced small
3 hard boiled eggs, roughly chopped
500 g (1 lb) prawns, shelled, deveined and chopped
1 white onion, finely chopped
¼ cup bread and butter cucumber, cut in strips
1 tablespoon finely chopped parsley
salt and pepper

Mix in a basin all above ingredients. The mixture should be well seasoned. Toss lightly with Tomato Mayonnaise. Place into lightly oiled basin (about 4 cup size). Press gently with the back of a spoon so there are no air bubbles. Chill until set. This usually takes about 2 hours.

Tomato Mayonnaise
3 teaspoons gelatine
2 tablespoons water
1 cup of an oil mayonnaise
2 tablespoons tomato sauce
1 tablespoon Worcestershire sauce
2 teaspoons horseradish relish

Mix the gelatine with cold water and stir. Dissolve over hot water. Mix together in a basin mayonnaise, tomato sauce, Worcestershire sauce and horseradish. Add gelatine and stir. Use immediately.

To Serve
6 thin slices fresh pineapple

Unmould the seafood on a platter. Cut the pineapple slices in half and remove cores. Arrange overlapping around the mould. Serve a portion of seafood on top of two half slices of pineapple.

Scallops Ravigote

500 g (1 lb) scallops
1 slice lemon
1 sprig parsley
½ cup water
1 cup white wine
little salt

Clean the scallops and separate the coral from the white part. Place lemon, parsley, water, wine and salt in a saucepan. Bring to the boil; add the white part of the scallop. Cook over gentle heat for 3 minutes; add the coral and cook 2 minutes. Remove and drain. One of the most important things about the dish is not to overcook the scallops or they become tough. Cut the white part into slices if large.

Sauce
½ cup olive or vegetable oil
3 tablespoons white vinegar
2 teaspoons capers, finely chopped
1 tablespoon finely chopped parsley
4 spring onions, finely chopped
1 hard boiled egg
1 teaspoon French mustard
salt and pepper to taste

Mix together the oil, vinegar, capers, parsley, and onions. Mash the hard boiled egg, add mustard and graduraly mix in oil and vinegar mixture. Season to taste. Mix the scallops with this sauce. They can be kept refrigerated for as long as 24 hours in the mixture. Remove and leave to stand at room temperature for about 30 minutes before serving or it is too thick. Serve with thinly sliced bread and butter. They look attractive served in small scallop shells.
As a variation this dish can be made using a mixture of seafood, prawns, crayfish and scallops. The sauce is enough for 500 g (1 lb) of seafood.

Prawn Pâté

Serves 4

250 g (½ lb) prawns
45 g (1½ oz) butter
½ small packet cream cheese (about 60 g or 2 oz)
1 tablespoon mayonnaise
few drops tabasco
good pinch nutmeg
1 small clove crushed garlic
2 teaspoons lemon juice

Shell and devein prawns. Mash the butter and cream cheese well until soft. Chop prawns very finely. Add the seasonings, tasting as you go. Pack into a small mould or dish. Serve with buttered toast or French bread. This improves by being made 6 hours before serving. Provided the prawns were fresh ones, it will keep refrigerated for several days.

Cold Salmon Mousse

Serves 8

I'm aware there are salmon mousse recipes featured in just about every book on the market, but with no attempt at being modest about it, this particular mousse is the best one I have ever eaten.

Two 220 g (7½ oz) tins best quality pink or red salmon
1 tablespoon gelatine
¼ cup water
1 tablespoon sugar
1 teaspoon dry, English-style mustard
½ teaspoon salt
½ cup white vinegar
1 tablespoon horseradish relish
1 tablespoon mayonnaise
1 cup finely diced celery
2 teaspoons chopped capers
2 tablespoons finely chopped spring onions
2 tablespoons bread and butter cucumber
½ cup cream, lightly whipped

Put the salmon through a *moulin*, mash or blend. If you put in the blender you will need to add the vinegar. Mix the gelatine and water together and stir; dissolve standing over hot water. Mix dissolved gelatine with sugar, mustard, salt, white vinegar, horseradish relish and mayonnaise and stir into salmon. Add the celery, capers, spring onion and bread and butter cucumber. Lastly fold through cream. Put into lightly oiled mould to set (4 cup size). Turn out on to a platter and serve with Cucumber Salad.
This keeps well for several days.

SALADS

To most people salad means simply tossed green salad, a variety of lettuce leaves moistened with a classic French dressing, the primary requisites being just very freshly crisped greens, a dressing that has been made from finest oil and vinegar and a little seasoning. And agreed, with a dinner or after a meat course, this is the best salad to serve to cleanse the palate. (Although many wine people feel the oil and vinegar dressing ruins the palate for tasting a top quality wine.)

This section is mostly devoted to salads which are variations of vegetables and some fruits, salads suitable for serving at parties or with meat for summer meals while others make an interesting first course.

Lettuce Salad with Mushroom Dressing

1 lettuce

Dressing
6 firm mushrooms
salt and pepper
1 teaspoon sugar
1 tablespoon lemon juice
4 spring onions, chopped finely
2 tablespoons sour cream
6 tablespoons oil
2 tablespoons vinegar
1 clove crushed garlic

Remove stalks from mushrooms and slice wafer thin. Sprinkle with salt, pepper and sugar, lemon juice. Add spring onions and sour cream. Mix together oil, vinegar, garlic and season with salt and pepper. Add the mushroom mixture to this and leave aside for an hour. Break the lettuce into bite-sized pieces and toss with dressing just before serving.

Green Salad with French Dressing

If necessary, wash the greens, but mostly apart from removing any grit in the root of a lettuce, it should be quite clean and makes a better salad if not washed. Break into pieces with your fingers and place in the refrigerator. If put into a metal bowl, such as a steam pudding basin, in the crisper, the coldness of the bowl will crisp them very quickly.

The type of oil is often a matter of personal taste, the flavour of olive oil varying in the different grades from light to strong and heavy. Many people now prefer a good quality peanut oil, and especially if you can get a French one, this has a light and nutty flavour.

Wine vinegar is a must or a good cider vinegar could be used, but malt vinegar is too strongly flavoured. The majority of books state firmly it should be mixed before using. I would disagree with this provided no extra seasonings such as herbs or garlic are added which definitely will spoil the flavour. It needs a good shaking again just before mixing with the greens. Only enough should be added so there is sufficient to coat the greens without leaving any on the bottom of the salad bowl after it is tossed.

French Dressing
½ teaspoon salt
a few grindings of pepper
2 tablespoons wine vinegar
6 tablespoons oil

Mix salt, pepper and vinegar together. Gradually beat in the oil; it should be thick. If you wish a pinch of dry mustard can be added.

Tomato Rice Salad

3 cups freshly cooked warm rice
3 ripe tomatoes, peeled
6 tablespoons oil
2 tablespoons white vinegar
½ teaspoon dry English-style mustard
½ teaspoon sugar
seasoning of salt and pepper
3 tablespoons finely chopped parsley

Place the rice in a large bowl. Make sure it is very well drained. Cut the peeled tomatoes into tiny pieces and mix with the warm rice. Mix oil, vinegar, mustard and sugar together. Stir into the rice and season well with salt and pepper. Stand until cooled and then stir through the parsley.

This salad has an attractive pink colour and very moist flavour. If you wish a clove of crushed garlic can also be added to the dressing.

Cauliflower Salad with Tuna Sauce

1 cauliflower, small to medium sized

Cook until just tender, drain well. Place in salad bowl, pour over Tuna Sauce and leave to cool. Serve when cold.

Tuna Sauce
220 g (7 oz) tin tuna
4 flat anchovy fillets, chopped
1 small white onion, finely diced
2 tablespoons capers, finely chopped
2 tablespoons parsley, finely chopped
2 hard boiled eggs
grated rind of 1 lemon
1 clove garlic, crushed
salt and pepper
¾ cup oil
¼ cup white vinegar

Mash tuna or put through *moulin*. Add anchovy fillets, onion, capers and parsley. Mash hard boiled eggs and add with lemon rind, garlic and a little salt and pepper. Mix the oil and vinegar together and add very slowly. It should form a thick sauce. The top can be garnished with a little extra chopped parsley if you wish.

Zucchini Salad

500 g (1 lb) small zucchini
1 small white onion
5 medium-sized button mushrooms
1 large ripe tomato
1 clove garlic, crushed
6 tablespoons oil
2 tablespoons white vinegar
¼ teaspoon salt
black pepper
¼ teaspoon sugar
¼ cup finely chopped parsley

Remove ends of zucchini and cut into very thin slices. Cook in salted water about 5 minutes or until just barely tender. Drain and run cold water over them until they are cool. Drain well. Slice onion wafer thin. Remove stalks from mushrooms and also cut into very wafer thin slices. Peel tomato and cut into small pieces. Mix onion, mushroom and tomato together. Mix oil, vinegar, garlic, salt, pepper and sugar together and stir into onion, mushroom and tomato mixture. Leave to stand about 1 hour. Mix this into cooled zucchini, add parsley and toss gently. It can be served immediately or left for several hours. Although the mushroom isn't cooked, it becomes soft when marinated in the dressing.

Potato Salad

Serves 4

500 g (1 lb) small new potatoes
1 white onion diced very finely
¼ cup olive oil
¼ cup dry white wine
1 tablespoon white vinegar
¼ cup finely chopped parsley
plenty of salt and pepper

Cook the potatoes in the skins and peel while warm. If the potatoes are small, leave whole. If larger, cut in thick slices. While still warm, mix with the onion, oil, wine, vinegar, parsley and season well. Toss gently. Leave to cool and it will absorb the flavour of the wine. It is excellent with ham or continental spiced sausage dishes. It can also be served as soon as it is made while still warm.

Welsh Salad

1 cup diced celery
½ cup diced green pepper
1 long cucumber, peeled, cut in halves and sliced thinly
½ cup sliced radishes
1 bunch spring onions, diced
3 ripe tomatoes, peeled and diced
about 6 stuffed green olives, sliced thinly

Mix all the above ingredients together and keep chilled. Before serving mix with dressing and toss well.

Dressing
½ cup peanut or olive oil
¼ cup white vinegar
1 teaspoon sugar
1 teaspoon dry, English-style mustard
1 tablespoon finely chopped mint
1 teaspoon salt

Mix all dressing ingredients together. This can be made some time beforehand. This salad is very colourful and refreshing to eat.

Tabbooli Salad (Bulgur Salad)

Serves 8

1½ cups bulgur
1 bunch very finely chopped spring onions
salt and pepper
1½ cups finely chopped parsley
½ cup olive oil
⅓ cup lemon juice
1 large ripe tomato, peeled

The bulgur can be bought in health food shops or some delicatessens. Quite often it is just labelled cracked wheat, sometimes wheat grist. The cracked wheat is slightly larger and coarser in texture but either makes a very good salad. Place the bulgur in a bowl and cover with cold water. Leave to stand for about 1 hour. Drain well and press out the excess water. Combine with the spring onions, add plenty of salt and pepper and then the parsley. Add oil and lemon juice. It should taste quite tart and fresh and sometimes this quantity of oil and lemon may need a slight adjustment. Put the salad in a bowl. Cut the tomato into tiny pieces and sprinkle over the top. If you like for a variation, a couple of tablespoons of finely chopped mint can be added as well as the parsley.

Salad Gwendoline

3 oranges cut in segments
1 large cucumber, skinned
salt

Cut the oranges without any pith or membrane. Skin the cucumber and cut into slices. Salt a little and let stand a couple of hours. Drain very well and mix with dressing just before serving.

Dressing
¼ cup sour cream
1 teaspoon chopped fresh mint
pinch salt
1 teaspoon sugar
1 small very finely chopped white onion

Mix the dressing ingredients and keep refrigerated. A little fresh mint chopped can be sprinkled on top. This is a refreshing salad with fish or steak.

Pineapple Rice Salad

Serves 8

1 medium-sized pineapple
¾ cup long grain rice
2 tablespoons sultanas
2 tablespoons peanuts
½ medium-sized green pepper, finely chopped
30 g (1 oz) butter
1 diced white onion
1 teaspoon curry powder
1 tablespoon mayonnaise
French Dressing

Cut the pineapple in halves lengthwise. Remove the flesh and cut into cubes, discarding the hard core. Cook the rice in a large pot of salted water and drain. Mix with sultanas, peanuts, green pepper and the pineapple. Melt the butter, sauté the onion until softened, add curry powder and cook a minute, stirring. Remove from the heat; add to the rice with the mayonnaise. Mix with enough French Dressing to make the mixture moist. This varies depending on the juiciness of the pineapple and moistness of the rice. Pile the salad up into the shells. Usually there is a bit more than can be fitted back into the pineapple shell. Do not chill this for the best flavour. It goes particularly well with ham or chicken dishes.

French Dressing
6 tablespoons olive or peanut oil
2 tablespoons white wine vinegar
pinch dry, English-style mustard
little salt and pepper

Do not use all of the above quantity, only enough to moisten.

PÂTÉS AND TERRINES

Is there a difference between a terrine and pâté? Mostly these words are used interchangeably by English and French — terrine meaning the deep, straight-sided dish (the word now includes the contents), whereas a pâté is rather more a paste or pastry covered dish. It doesn't really seem to matter nowadays. The important thing is the flavour and texture of the finished product. They are not always so inexpensive when containing pork, livers, brandies and spices, but are fine to have on hand for cold meals requiring only crusty bread and salads to make a feast.

They can be cooked in any type of baking dish. It can be oval or rectangular but the best materials to use are porcelain, pottery or ovenglass. Be careful not to overcook the meat. It is done when it appears to be floating in its own fat, or when a knitting or larding needle is stuck in the centre and comes out clean.

Chicken Liver Pâté

Serves 8

This is a very rich but fine pâté. Quantities can be halved if you wish, although it will keep for a week covered in the refrigerator.

500 g (1 lb) chicken livers
½ cup Madeira
90 g (3 oz) butter
1 small white onion, very finely chopped
⅓ cup cream
2 teaspoons lemon juice
salt and pepper
allspice
thyme

Trim the chicken livers and cut in half. Place in a bowl and cover with Madeira. Leave for 2 hours, stirring once or twice. Drain the livers, keep the liquid. Heat a frying pan, melt 30 g (1 oz) butter and cook livers and onion until they are browned on the outside but still slightly pink inside. Transfer to a bowl. Add the Madeira liquid to the pan and stir any little brown pieces from the bottom. If the pan is not a large one, cook the livers in two separate batches. Put all this through a *moulin* or blend. Melt the remaining 60 g (2 oz) butter and add gradually with the cream. Season with lemon, salt, pepper, allspice and thyme to taste. It must be very smooth; if not sieve it. Fill a mould and chill, covered. It has a better flavour if kept 24 hours before eating. If keeping, pour a thin layer of clarified butter over the top.

Country Terrine

Serves 8

250 g (½ lb) fillet of veal
1 tablespoon brandy
250 g (½ lb) bacon, rind removed
30 g (1 oz) butter
1 white onion, finely diced
3 tablespoons port
500 g (1 lb) pork, minced ⎫ **These can be minced together by the butcher**
250 g (½ lb) veal, minced ⎭
2 eggs
1 clove garlic, crushed
½ cup finely chopped parsley
1 teaspoon salt
black pepper

Cut veal into strips and place in a basin, pour brandy over and stand for ½ hour. You need a terrine dish or casserole with a lid, about 5 cup size. Line the dish with bacon on the base and sides. Keep aside 2 strips for the top of the terrine. Melt butter, sauté onion until softened. Add port and leave to cook until slightly reduced. Place minced pork and veal in a basin and add port and onion. Add eggs, garlic, parsley, salt and pepper. Drain brandy from the veal strips and add liquid to the minced meat. Beat well. Place ⅓ of the force meat on the base of the terrine dish. Add half the veal strips, then repeat this and cover finally with remaining layer of force meat. Cover the top with the bacon you kept aside and place 1 bay leaf on top. Cover with foil, then put on the lid. Stand this in a dish of hot water to reach about halfway up the terrine. Cook 1¼ hours in a moderate oven, 180-190°C (350-375°F). It will come away from the sides when cooked. Leave to stand for about ½ hour to settle, then put a light weight on top and leave to cool. Chill. It has a better flavour if left for 24 hours before eating and keeps well for 5 days.

Terrine of Pork

This terrine keeps well for 3 to 4 days.

60 g (2 oz) butter
1 large white onion, finely diced
1 egg
1 tablespoon finely chopped parsley
grated rind of 1 lemon
1 cup breadcrumbs made from stale bread
1 teaspoon salt
black pepper
250 g (½ lb) minced veal
3 small pork fillets each about 250 g (½ lb)
16 prunes, stones removed
2 tablespoons dry sherry

You can use either a pâté crock for this or a loaf tin about a 4 cup size. Melt the butter and sauté the onion until softened. Mix in a large basin the egg, parsley, lemon rind, breadcrumbs, salt, pepper and veal. Add the cooked onion to this and mix well. Cut each pork fillet through the centre leaving it joined on one side. Flatten lightly. Place 1 pork fillet in the dish and top with a thin layer of the stuffing. Arrange about 4 prunes down the centre, put another fillet on top and then more stuffing. Repeat this until all is used up but top layer must be pork fillet. Pour the sherry over the top. Cover pâté with foil and then a lid, if it is a pâté crock, or if a loaf tin, just a double thickness of foil will do. Bake in a moderate oven, 180-190°C (350-375°F), standing in a tin of water to come halfway up, for about 1½ hours. Leave to cool slightly. Then put a plate or board and a weight on top. Leave for several hours or until cold. Keep refrigerated. This terrine is best sliced thickly as otherwise it tends to separate slightly.

SUMMER CHICKEN DISHES

Cold chicken dishes usually fall into one of two categories — very nice or very nasty. Cooked chicken, being one of the most perishable of all foods, needs to be kept well refrigerated and unfortunately often becomes rather firm and dry in the process. If it has been gently simmered in liquid, it can be left in this liquid but obviously is rather unspectacular served this way. One of the best ways of preparing it is by covering it with a sauce, so it can be kept chilled without any risk of dryness and yet prepared beforehand for serving as a summer dish.

Cold Chicken in Mustard Sauce

Although this is a mustard sauce, it is not particularly hot; it has a delicate colour and flavour and keeps the chicken very moist.

Mustard Mixture
1 teaspoon dry, English-style mustard
enough water to mix it to a paste
1 tablespoon French mustard
1 teaspoon white vinegar
1 large chicken 2 kg (4 lb) (or 2 small ones if you prefer)

Mix the mustards together with the vinegar. Rub the skin of the chicken with the mustard and leave refrigerated for 24 hours.
To Cook: Cover the chicken with a large piece of buttered foil. Place in casserole or baking dish. Pour 3 cups water into the dish, adding a little salt. Place in a moderate oven, 180-190°C (350-375°F), and cook in the foil until quite tender. Keep liquid; skim fat from the top.

Sauce
30 g (1 oz) butter
1 tablespoon plain flour
1½ cups chicken stock
3 tablespoons cream
1 quantity of above mustard mixture

Melt the butter, add flour and cook 1 minute. Add stock and stir constantly until thickened. Cook a few minutes and then add cream and check for seasoning. Mix this gradually into the quantity of mustard mixture and leave to cool. Cut the chicken into pieces and arrange on a platter. Spoon the mustard sauce over the top and leave to set. Decorate with chopped parsley and keep cold. This will set quite firmly.

Cold Chicken in Curried Cream

Serves 8

2 cooked chickens, about 1.5 kg (3 lb) in size.

These can be steamed or gently boiled but be sure to keep them refrigerated in liquid so they will not be dry for the salad. Skin and divide into portions

Sauce
3 tablespoons vegetable oil
2 medium-sized white onions, roughly diced
1 tablespoon curry powder
¼ cup tomato sauce
1 tablespoon apricot jam
1 tablespoon paw paw and mango chutney
½ cup oil mayonnaise
½ cup cream, lightly whipped

Heat the oil and add the onions, cook until softened. Add curry powder and cook a minute. Remove from the heat, add tomato sauce and apricot jam. If the jam has pieces of fruit in it chop these small or push through a sieve. Add chutney last. Leave to cool. When cold fold into the oil mayonnaise and lastly stir through the whipped cream. Place a little of the mixture on the base of a serving dish. Arrange the chicken over this and then top with the remainder of the sauce. There should be enough to coat each portion of chicken. Keep refrigerated. It can be kept 12 hours like this and the chicken will keep very moist in the sauce.

SUMMER VEGETABLES, SOME HOT, SOME COLD

Cucumbers

Nothing could be more summery and refreshing than cucumber salad or cucumber in sandwiches but don't disregard its uses as a hot vegetable. It has a delicate flavour and when served plain either as a side dish or stuffed makes an interesting entrée or luncheon dish.

Stuffed Cucumbers

3 small cucumbers

Peel the cucumbers, cut in half lengthwise and place in a saucepan of cold salted water. Bring to the boil; simmer covered for about 5 minutes or until slightly softened. Drain, rinse with cold water and drain again. Remove the seeds using a teaspoon.

Filling
45 g (1½ oz) butter
1 white onion, finely diced
125 g (4 oz) mushrooms, finely sliced
½ cup breadcrumbs, made from stale bread
2 tablespoons cream
1 cup finely diced chicken
250 g (½ lb) cooked prawns, shelled, deveined and finely chopped
salt and pepper

Melt butter and sauté onion and mushroom until softened. Place breadcrumbs in a bowl, add cream and mix well. Add onion and mushroom mixture to this with chicken and prawns. Season well with salt and pepper. Mash well with a fork so it binds together. Fill the cucumbers with this mixture. Place in buttered ovenproof dish. Cover the top with buttered foil and bake in a moderate oven, 180-190°C (350-375°F), about 25 minutes.

Topping
125 g (4 oz) cream cheese
1 large egg
¼ cup finely diced or grated gruyère cheese
salt and pepper

Mash the cream cheese in a bowl. Add egg and gruyère, seasoning with a little salt and pepper. Spoon this over the top of the filling. Bake another 5 minutes. If you aren't keen on hot cucumber, then the same dish can be made using zucchini. Don't cook the zucchini first, but just cut in half and scoop out the seeds using a teaspoon. As long as the zucchini are not too large and are very fresh, they cook through in the same time. If boiled first, they go limp and collapse a bit when baked.

Baked Cucumbers

4 large cucumbers
1 tablespoon white vinegar
1 teaspoon salt
1 teaspoon sugar

Peel cucumbers and cut in long slithers discarding the centre seedy part. Place the cucumber strips in a bowl and sprinkle with the vinegar, salt and sugar. Stand for about 1 hour. Drain well. Place them in an ovenproof dish.

60 g (2 oz) melted butter
½ bunch spring onions, finely chopped
black pepper

Melt the butter and pour over the cucumbers. Stir a little. Add the spring onion and black pepper and cook uncovered in a moderate oven, 180-190°C (350-375°F), for about ½ an hour, stirring occasionally. This can be cooked beforehand and then reheated for about 10 minutes.

Capsicum Peppers

The capsicum peppers comprise a diverse group of plants, used both as vegetables and spices, peppers of every conceivable shape and size, some are long, conical, round, crooked, others like beans. They can be as small as a pea or else as large as the sweet, large green bell pepper. The colours range from green, red, orange to yellow. They can be fiery or bland. Generally, it is a safe rule the smaller the pepper, the hotter, while the large ones have no trace of heat. Virtually every country in the world with a tropical or semi-tropical, or a warm and long summer season, grow varieties of the capsicum and it has made a strong impact on the cooking of many countries.

Pineapple Alexandra (see p. 65)

When cutting them up raw it is much easier and quicker to cut them on the dull side. The shiny side has a tough skin which makes it much harder to slice. Be sure too to remove the small cluster of seeds in the centre.

Mediterranean Stuffed Peppers

Cut 2 large or 3 medium-sized peppers in half. Remove seeds: cut in chunky pieces ready to stuff (size about 5 x 5 cm or 2 x 2 inch). They shrink a little when cooked but the pieces should be just a nice size to put on top of slices of French bread stick.

Mix Together in a Bowl
2 large ripe tomatoes, peeled, seeded and cut in small pieces
1 tin anchovy fillets (45 g) (1½ oz) and the oil from the tin
4 tablespoons breadcrumbs, made from stale bread
1 large clove crushed garlic
a little black pepper
1 teaspoon sugar

It should be quite salty enough with the anchovies so don't add any extra.
Mix well; it should be just firm enough to hold a shape. Place a little of this in each piece of pepper. Put in a shallow, oiled ovenproof dish. On top of each one place a tiny piece of butter, the size of a pea. Bake 25 minutes in a moderate oven, 180-190°C (350-375°F). Leave to cool and serve on slices of buttered bread stick as an appetizer. Just don't breathe too heavily after you've eaten these!

Peppers in Cream

2 large green peppers
1 large red pepper
2 white onions
60 g (2 oz) butter
1 teaspoon flour
½ cup cream
2 tablespoons white wine
¼ teaspoon tabasco
salt

Cut the peppers down and into long strips, not too thickly. Cut the onion into half slices. Melt the butter and gently sauté the pepper and onion until softened. Add the flour and leave to fry a minute; then add cream, wine, seasonings. Cook over low heat for about 10 minutes. This is excellent served with steak dishes and can be made beforehand and reheated. If it goes too thick, just add a little more cream or a tablespoon of milk.

Marinaded Peppers

3 red peppers
3 green peppers
6 spring onions, finely chopped
3 tablespoons oil
1 tablespoon red wine vinegar
salt and pepper
½ teaspoon paprika

The combination of red and green peppers is used mainly for colour in the salad rather than for any difference to the flavour. Cut the peppers in half. Remove the seedy part and flatten them slightly. Place under a preheated griller until the skin has bubbled and is a golden colour. Remove and then let them cool slightly. Peel

Pineapple Rice Salad (see p. 44), Tabbooli Salad (see p. 43)

away the skin which is a bit like tissue paper. The smokey flavour the grilling gives to the peppers is one of the main features of this dish. Cut the peppers into thick strips. Place in a bowl and mix with the spring onions. Mix together oil, vinegar, salt, pepper and paprika and pour over peppers. Stir and leave to stand for about 8 hours before serving. They are best served at room temperature. This can be served as part of an hors d'oeuvre platter or a first course with thin slices of ham.

Corn

The freshest corn tastes the best; nobody will disagree with this, but it isn't always possible to have the rows of green and gold throughout the garden. Purists advise before plucking that you have the water boiling. You then put on your running shoes, pluck the ears of corn and race to the kitchen, frantically trimming the husks along the route. Interesting suggestion, but unrealistic, and unfortunately, most of the bought corn has been picked a day before eating. Still, if firm and fresh-looking, it is a delight.

BASIC METHOD OF COOKING: Remove the top, casing leaves and silk. Boil in a large saucepan of water for about 15 minutes. Do not salt the water when cooking as this toughens the corn. The best way to eat it is dripping with butter and seasoned with salt and pepper. Small holders can be bought which are inserted in both ends, although for some reason it seems to taste better just held in your hands. Though it must be admitted that butter dripping down to the elbows is not very elegant at a dinner, so it is more a dish for the kitchen table.

Summer Sweet Corn Medley

60 g (2 oz) butter
2 rashers diced bacon
1 small green pepper
1 large diced white onion
4 small corn cobs
salt and pepper
1 tablespoon cream
2 tablespoons tasty cheese, grated finely

Melt butter, cook bacon, pepper and onion until softened. Cut corn away from the cob, using a sharp knife. Add to pan with salt and pepper, cover and cook over low heat about 15 minutes. Before serving add cream and cheese. Stir until cheese melts. This goes well with chicken or can be served as a light luncheon dish accompanied by toast fingers.

Egg-plant

The exotic egg-plant captured the imagination and palates of the mysterious East and Near East centuries ago. When it first appeared in Britain, the early botanists decided because of its family connection with the deadly nightshade, it was a sinister vegetable, causing insanity or even death. It was actually called 'mad apple' or 'raging apple'. It took many years before the superstition vanished and it became accepted, despite the fact that it was eaten so extensively in southern Asia and the Near East. We are mostly familiar with the satiny purple variety. There are types that are yellow, white and even striped. It can be egg shaped, long as a cucumber or as round as a tomato.

BASIC PREPARATION: Egg-plant has considerable water content. It is best if this is removed first. Cut into slices or cubes. Sprinkle with a little salt and leave to stand for about 20 minutes. Drain away the liquid. The salting also removes the slightly bitter taste in the egg-plant.

Egg-plant Salad

1 large egg-plant (about 500 g or 1 lb altogether)
a little salt
a little peanut oil
1 large white onion, finely diced
2 tablespoons tomato purée
2 teaspoons sugar
1 tablespoon white vinegar
2 tablespoons chopped parsley
2 teaspoons chopped capers
½ tin anchovy fillets, chopped (approx. 2 teaspoons)

Peel the egg-plant, dice and sprinkle with salt. Leave to stand for 1 hour. Drain well. Cover the base of a frying pan with a thin film of oil; heat and cook the egg-plant until softened. If you have only a small pan, it may be best to do this in two batches. Remove. Cook the onion in the oil until soft; add tomato purée and sugar. Return the egg-plant and stir it until coated with the sauce; add vinegar and cook 1 minute. Remove to a bowl; add the parsley, capers and anchovy and taste as it must be well seasoned. Cool and keep chilled. It is served cold with toast as an appetizer and keeps well for 1 week. This mixture should not be too wet and if you find when preparing it the pan has a lot of liquid, turn up and heat and cook until it has boiled away.

Casserole of Egg-plant

2 medium-sized egg-plants
salt
a little oil
60 g (2 oz) butter
2 medium-sized white onions, sliced thinly
250 g (½ lb) mushrooms, sliced thinly
500 g (1 lb) tomatoes, sliced thinly
salt and pepper
1 large clove garlic, crushed

Slice the egg-plant, leaving skin on. Salt and leave to stand for about 1 hour, then drain. Heat the oil and fry the egg-plant until golden on all sides. This takes a while and you often need to add a little extra oil to the pan as you go. Remove and leave aside on kitchen paper to drain. Melt 30 g (1 oz) of the butter and cook the white onions until soft and just turning golden. Remove. Melt the remaining 30 g (1 oz) of butter, add the mushrooms, a little pepper and salt and leave these to cook a few minutes until softened. Remove and place aside. Grease an ovenproof casserole (7 cup size). Place in a layer of egg-plant; season with salt and pepper. Then dot a few little bits of crushed garlic over this. Add a layer of onion and a layer of mushroom and cover this with slices of tomato. Repeat until all the ingredients are used up, seasoning well as you go. Usually it makes about 3 layers of egg-plant. It is best if the last layer is sliced tomato.
This casserole can be prepared beforehand and left in the refrigerator for 6 hours. Bake for about ½ hour in the centre of a moderate oven, 180-190°C (350-375°F).

THE TOMATO

Tomatoes form an indispensable and influential item in our diets. After all who could imagine our national Australian dish, the meat pie, without a generous blob of the stuff oozing out.

For many years after it was first brought to England people didn't dare to try the fruit. It was believed to be lethal, or at the very least 'lust provoking'. People who wanted to try the fruit for it's lust-provoking properties became nervous about it when a European botanist identified it as a member of the deadly nightshade family. Strangely enough however, peppers and potatoes were eaten and these also have branches in the nightshade family tree — their flowers are suggestive of the nightshade blooms — but somehow they escaped all the stigma. It was believed eating one of these fruits would strike you dead or at the very least tempt the devil. For three hundred years after its discovery it was used just as an ornament or curiosity and it was well into the nineteenth century before it was really appreciated. It would be difficult now to imagine life without this sun-ripened red ball of vitamin C.

Tomato and Egg Salad with Sardine Dressing

4 hard boiled eggs
6 ripe tomatoes
1 tin 125 g (4 oz) sardines
6 tablespoons oil
2 tablespoons white wine vinegar
2 teaspoons grated onion
2 teaspoons lemon juice
salt and pepper
2 tablespoons mayonnaise
¼ cup finely chopped parsley

Shell the eggs and cut in slices. Peel the tomatoes and cut in slices also. Arrange a layer of eggs on a platter. Place tomato slices on top. Mash the sardines well. Mix together oil, vinegar, grated onion, lemon juice, salt and pepper. Lastly, stir in mayonnaise and parsley. Add to sardines gradually and pour this over the tomato. Leave to stand for about ½ hour before serving but it can be kept for about 4 hours.
Serve with a little extra parsley on top and crusty bread as a first course.

Stuffed Tomato Cups

30 g (1 oz) butter
2 tablespoons pine nuts (obtainable in health food shops or delicatessen)
1 onion
8 medium-sized mushrooms
1 cup finely diced cooked chicken
2 tablespoons breadcrumbs
1 tablespoon sultanas
1 small egg
1 tablespoon cream
salt and pepper
6 medium-sized (to large) ripe tomatoes
a little vegetable oil

Melt a tiny piece of butter the size of a pea and toss the pine nuts until golden. Place in a basin. Melt the remaining butter and sauté onion. Chop up two of the mushrooms and cook for a moment with the onion, seasoning with salt and pepper. Place this in with the pine nuts. Add chicken, breadcrumbs, sultanas, egg and cream, seasoning well. Cut the tops from the tomatoes and carefully remove centres. Season. Turn upside down to drain. Fill with chicken mixture. Remove stalks from the remaining mushrooms and brush the tops with a little vegetable oil, salt and pepper. Place one of these on top of each tomato. Bake in a moderate oven, 180-190°C (350-375°F), for 15 minutes or until filling is set and tomato cooked. This dish makes an attractive entrée or light luncheon dish.

Tomatoes in Cream	500 g (1 lb) small ripe but firm tomatoes 30 g (1 oz) butter ¼ teaspoon salt, little black pepper ½ teaspoon sugar 1 teaspoon fresh chopped basil or a pinch dried basil ¼ cup cream

Peel the tomatoes by plunging into boiling water for 30 seconds and remove the skins. Slice tomatoes thickly. Remove some of the seeds. Melt the butter, add tomatoes, and season with salt, pepper, sugar and basil. Cook a moment, turning once until just slightly softened. Add the cream and simmer gently for a couple of minutes.

Baked Tomatoes with Breadcrumb Topping	6 small ripe tomatoes salt and pepper sprinkle of sugar 3 tablespoons finely chopped parsley ½ cup breadcrumbs 1 clove crushed garlic 60 g (2 oz) butter

Cut the tomatoes in half. Sprinkle with salt, pepper and sugar and turn upside down. Leave for 30 minutes to drain. Mix together in a bowl the parsley, breadcrumbs, garlic, and a little salt and pepper. Press some of the topping on each tomato half. Melt the butter and trickle a little over the top of each one. Bake in a buttered, shallow, ovenproof dish in a moderate oven, 180-190°C (350-375°F), for about 10 minutes.

STRAWBERRIES AND RASPBERRIES

Strawberries

With modern methods, the strawberry has become larger in size and the season longer. However, sometimes these out-of-season berries lack flavour. Nothing can really compare with ripe, fresh strawberries at the peak of their season. Then they really need nothing more when serving than a little castor sugar and cream and sometimes not even that is necessary.

For several summers we stayed in a beachside house with a beautiful orchard and gardens, including a large strawberry patch. Each morning, before the birds could feast for the day, we crawled up and down the lines picking the ripe berries. About half the quantity reached the kitchen, the remainder were eaten to 'keep up our strength'. The taste of those scented berries warm from the morning sunshine was something never forgotten — a flavour which can't be found in greengrocery-bought punnets. It would have been sacrilege to do anything except eat them simply on their own, but for times of the year when berries are not at their absolute best, different ways of serving them are needed — ways to bring out a little extra flavour and make them more exciting for serving as a dessert.

They are delicate fruit and, if clean, are best just brushed with a pastry brush. If you feel it is necessary to wash them, do it carefully. Don't put in a sieve and pour cold water over them as they bruise easily. It is far better to fill a basin with cold water and drop them in gently. The dirt falls out of the berries into the bottom of the basin and they remain undamaged. They can then be placed on kitchen paper to drain and kept refrigerated.

Strawberries with Champagne Cream

1 punnet of strawberries (or 2 if they are small punnets)
¾ cup champagne
3 tablespoons castor sugar
1 teaspoon grated orange rind
1 cup cream
4 extra tablespoons champagne

Hull the strawberries. Place in a bowl with the champagne, sugar and orange rind. Leave to stand for about 1 hour. Whip the cream until very stiff. Drain away ½ cup of the juices which will have collected around the berries. Gradually add this to the cream. Lastly add the extra champagne. This gives the cream a refreshing and slightly sharper taste. Serve the berries in the base of a champagne glass and top with the cream. If you need the glasses to drink the remainder of the champagne, serve the dessert in any small glass dishes. The type of champagne glasses for this would be the older, shallow type of champagne glass.

Glazed Strawberries

45 g (1½ oz) butter
3 tablespoons sugar
2 tablespoons brandy
2 tablespoons orange-flavoured liqueur
⅓ cup red currant jelly
juice 1 large orange
1 punnet strawberries

Melt the butter and add sugar. Cook until foaming but not brown. Add brandy, orange liqueur, red currant jelly and orange juice. Warm, stirring, until the jelly is melted. Add strawberries last. If large they are best cut in half. Only cook long enough to warm them through. They become very acidic if overcooked.
Serve with ice cream or it can be used as a sauce for crêpes.

Strawberry Hope Sauce

2 tablespoons castor sugar
1 teaspoon cornflour
4 tablespoons water
pulp of 3 passionfruit
1 box strawberries
2 tablespoons brandy (optional)

Put sugar and cornflour in a saucepan and add water gradually. Bring to a boil and add the passionfruit pulp. Remove. Leave to cool. Add strawberries several hours before serving. Add brandy just before serving. Serve with cream or ice cream.

Strawberries in Caramel Sauce

2 punnets of strawberries
60 g (2 oz) butter
2 tablespoons brown sugar
grated rind of 1 orange
juice of 1 orange
3 tablespoons cream
2 tablespoons brandy

If the strawberries are large, cut in half. Melt the butter, add the sugar and cook a moment until a pale golden colour. Add the orange rind and juice, and cook until the sugar is dissolved. Add the cream, then strawberries and warm through. Do not overcook strawberries or they become acidic in taste. Warm the brandy separately and light. Pour this over the top and serve plain or with ice cream.

Coêur à la Crême

250 g (½ lb) cream cheese
2 tablespoons icing sugar
½ teaspoon vanilla
pinch salt
½ cup cream
1 egg white

Beat cream cheese until soft. Add sugar and vanilla, a pinch of salt and mix well. Whip cream and egg white separately then fold together. Add to cream cheese. Press mixture into a small mould (about 2 cup size) lined with plastic wrap. Chill 24 hours or it can be frozen if you wish.
Serve with strawberries or raspberries.

Strawberry and Cream Cheese Tart

Pastry
1 cup plain flour
90 g (3 oz) soft butter
2 tablespoons icing sugar
1 egg yolk
½ teaspoon vanilla essence

Sift flour and make a well in the centre; add the soft butter, icing sugar, egg yolk and vanilla. Mix the centre ingredients together and then gradually work in the flour from the edges. Knead until soft. If a little sticky to use chill for a short time. Roll out to make a round circle the size of a large dinner plate (23 cm or 9 inch). Place this on a buttered scone tray and bake in a moderate oven, 180-190°C (350-375°F), about 20 minutes or until a light golden colour. Leave to cool and then remove and store in an airtight tin.

Cream Cheese Filling
125 g (4 oz) pkt cream cheese
2 tablespoons icing sugar
rind of 1 large orange finely grated

Mash cream cheese and add icing sugar and then orange rind. Spread a layer of this over the biscuit circle.

2 punnets strawberries
½ cup red currant jelly
½ cup cream

The best strawberries for this tart are small ones. If you can only buy the very large strawberries cut them in half and lay the cut side flat on the tart. Cover the base with berries to form even circles.

Warm the red currant jelly and when smooth coat the top of the berries, using a pastry brush. If any jelly is remaining, spoon into the gaps between them. This will keep well for about 6 hours then the base starts to lose its crispness.

Before serving, whip the cream until stiff and pipe a layer of rosettes around the edge. This really doesn't need any extra cream as the cheese filling is quite rich enough on its own.

Angel Mousse

This mousse can be served over any fresh fruits and is especially good with raspberries or strawberries.

Place a layer of fruit in small individual dishes or in shallow champagne glasses and then fill to the top with mousse.

3 eggs
4 tablespoons castor sugar
1 tablespoon brandy
1 tablespoon sweet sherry
1 tablespoon orange curacao
2 teaspoons gelatine
2 tablespoons cold water
½ cup cream

Separate the eggs and beat the yolks and castor sugar until thick. Add the brandy, sweet sherry, and orange curacao. Soften the gelatine with the cold water and dissolve over hot water. Beat the egg whites until very stiff. Fold the yolk and liqueur-mixture into the whites. Whip the cream until it holds a shape and fold through last.

Fills 6 individual dishes or 8 champagne glasses.

Chocolate Strawberry Delight

Cake
3 large eggs, separated
3 tablespoons sugar
2 tablespoons cocoa
½ teaspoon cinnamon
½ teaspoon vanilla essence
¼ teaspoon almond essence

Beat egg yolks and sugar until thick. Sift in cocoa and cinnamon and beat again. Add vanilla and almond essence. Beat egg whites until very stiff. Fold in half first, then the remaining half. Butter a sponge tin (20 cm) and gently tip in mixture. Bake in a moderate oven, 180-190°C (350-375°F), for 16-18 minutes. It puffs up during the cooking but settles as it cools. Leave a couple of minutes before turning out of the tin. This is a very light and fragile cake and can be kept in an airtight tin for several days.

Filling
1 cup cream
1 punnet strawberries
45 g (1½ oz) dark chocolate
15 g (½ oz) butter

Whip the cream and spread a thin layer over the top of the cake. Use about ¼ cup. Slice the strawberries and arrange on top of the cream. Break the chocolate into pieces. Melt the butter and when hot add the chocolate. Remove immediately from the heat and stir until chocolate is melted. Leave to cool a little and stir into the remaining cream. Spread or pipe this over the strawberries leaving an uncovered circle in the centre so they can be seen. If you wish, the top can also be dusted with a little extra grated chocolate.

This will keep refrigerated for 12 hours

Raspberry

This is a 'here today and gone tomorrow' fruit which was not even cultivated until four centuries ago and then only in small quantities. While they have a delicious fragrance and subtle flavour, raspberries and cream have never really attained the popularity of strawberries and cream. They bruise easily, are very fragile and need to be kept in a cool place and eaten fairly soon after picking.

My happiest memories of raspberries come from a holiday in France during the berry season. After dinner at night, a large crystal bowl of cold berries would be placed on the table, alongside a shaker of castor sugar and beside that a jug of thick cream. Nothing could be more perfect after a large meal. Perhaps it seems like gilding the lily to suggest other ways, but here are some other summery ideas.

Raspberry Brûlée

1 punnet raspberries
3 tablespoons castor sugar (quantity really depends on the sweetness of the berries)
3 tablespoons kirsch (If you don't have kirsch, the next best is an orange-flavoured liqueur.)
1 cup cream
light brown sugar

Place the raspberries in a small soufflé dish (4 to 5 cup capacity). Sprinkle with the castor sugar and kirsch. Stand 1 hour and stir gently once or twice.
Whip the cream until stiff and spread over the top. Chill for a couple of hours.
Before serving, sift a layer of brown sugar over the top of the cream. This shouldn't be too thick. Preheat the griller and place the dish underneath. Grill until the top is bubbling and caramelized. Serve immediately.

Raspberry Summer Pudding

This is an old and favourite way of using raspberries. I have included it as it has such a beautiful flavour; it is difficult to think of a nicer way to serve them.

500 g (1 lb) fresh raspberries
½ cup curacao
1 cup castor sugar
24 sponge fingers

Place the berries in a large bowl; add the curacao and sugar. Leave to stand about 1 hour or until there is quite a lot of liquid in the bowl.
Use a mould or pudding basin for this, one with a capacity of about 4 cups. Drain the berries and stir the juice well to make sure the sugar is dissolved. Dip the sponge fingers one at a time in the juice. The best variety of fingers are the dried out type rather than the very soft fresh ones. The soft ones tend to fall to pieces when soaked in the juice. Line the sides and then the base of the mould with sponge fingers. Cut them if they are not the right size. Place a few berries in the base, some more dipped fingers, and then another layer of berries. Repeat until all the fruit and sponge fingers are used. The top layer must be sponge. Place a piece of greaseproof paper on top or plastic wrap, then a plate and a weight about 500 g (1 lb). Place in refrigerator for about 12 hours. If you haven't used all the juices from the berries, place in a jug to serve with the pudding. Turn out on to a plate.

To Serve
1 cup cream
1 tablespoon castor sugar
½ teaspoon vanilla essence

Whip cream, add sugar and vanilla. Spread a layer over the outside of the pudding. Keep chilled. Once the cream is over this, use within about 6 hours.

Raspberry Baskets

*Makes 8 or 10
small baskets*

⅓ cup plain flour
⅓ cup icing sugar
4 tablespoons melted butter
1 egg white, stiffly beaten

Mix plain flour and icing sugar together. Add the melted butter and stir the mixture. Add the egg white and stir until it is a soft mixture.

Butter and lightly flour a scone tray and shake to get rid of the excess flour. Put about 2 or 3 teaspoons of mixture on the tray. Using a knife, spread it out into a thin circle. This is a rather slow job. If you find the knife sticks to the mixture, dip it into hot water, shake away the excess water and it is then much easier to spread. Also, when the trays become warmed as you are cooking the circles, they spread out with the warmth and this makes it easier. Bake in a moderate oven, 180-190°C (350-375°F), for about 5 minutes or until they are golden in colour. Remove immediately using a spatula and place either into the base of a cup or a small soufflé dish (size about 8 cm or 3 inch). There is no need to grease these. Press gently against the sides to form a small basket shape. They will firm up very quickly. Leave a moment and then remove. They can be stored in an airtight tin for about 5 days. They are very crisp and slightly fragile, so handle carefully.

NOTE: If the mixture is too thick and they crack when moulding into the baskets, add an extra tablespoon of butter. The baskets must be filled with the Raspberry Chocolate Cream mixture only at the last minute or they become soft and the flavour combination of the crisp basket with soft tart filling is ruined. The cream mixture can be prepared a couple of hours beforehand and kept refrigerated.

If you find these baskets too difficult to handle, serve the cream in small dishes or champagne glasses and top with raspberries. Make the biscuits up into small flat circles and serve alongside the dessert.

The baskets can also be filled with various ice creams and are delicious with strawberries and cream.

Raspberry Chocolate Cream Filling
1 punnet of raspberries
2 tablespoons castor sugar
1 tablespoon orange flavoured liqueur
½ cup cream
½ teaspoon vanilla
30 g (1 oz) dark chocolate

Place half the raspberries in a bowl. Add castor sugar and liqueur and stand for about 20 minutes.

Whip cream until stiff and add vanilla essence. Grate the chocolate finely and fold into cream, then add raspberries. Spoon some of this filling into each case and top with a tablespoon of the remaining fresh berries.

Raspberry Nut Torte

This cake base is very quick and simple to make and it is as light as a feather. It keeps moist for several days in an airtight tin.

Cake
125 g (4 oz) hazelnuts, finely ground (you can also use walnuts for a change)
grated rind of 2 lemons
1 tablespoon breadcrumbs made from stale white bread
5 large eggs, separated
1 cup castor sugar

Grease 2 sponge tins (size 20 cm or 8 inch). Line the base with a circle of greaseproof paper and grease again. Mix nuts, lemon rind and breadcrumbs together. Beat egg yolks with castor sugar until thick and lemon in colour. Beat egg whites until stiff. Fold whites gently into egg yolks. Lastly add the nut mixture and fold through. Divide mixture between the tins and bake in a moderate oven, 180-190°C (350-375°F), for 16-20 minutes or until just firm on top.

Filling
1½ cups cream
3 tablespoons castor sugar
½ teaspoon vanilla
1 tablespoon rum
1 punnet fresh raspberries (about 1 cup)

Whip the cream until stiff. Add sugar, vanilla and rum. Beat for a second. Roughly crush the berries with a fork and gently fold in. The cream will turn a delicate shade of pink. Spread a thick layer on one of the cakes, top with the other cake. Spread top and sides with the remaining cream. If you wish you can save about 10 raspberries and use to decorate the top of the cake.
Leave for 1 hour for the flavours to mature, although it will keep like this for 12 hours, refrigerated.
When raspberries are out of season, the same cake can be made using a punnet of strawberries. Crush these just the same before adding to the cream.

PEACHES AND APRICOTS

Peaches

The Latin word for peach tree, *persicus*, simply means Persian and relates to the origin of the fruit. It is actually of Chinese origin and they grew oval, round and even flattened peaches, with yellow, white or red flesh. In folklore they were rich in symbolism, signifying immortality and longevity, while peach blossoms were associated with promiscuity and peach growers carefully avoided planting any tree near the windows of a lady's boudoir.

In France the fruit was grown from earliest times and French peaches are amongst the best in the world. The peaches of Montreuil, now a suburb of France have been considered among the choicest in France since the early 1700s. Here the walled gardens were planted on both sides with the fan-shaped peach trees, trained in espaliers, the whitewashed walls setting off the masses of delicate pink flowers. Iron hooks and rivets were put in to secure the trees to the walls to keep the fruit-laden branches from collapsing. The ladies and gentlemen of Versailles walked these paths, while artists and their models wandered along in search of inspiration. These priceless peaches were transported all over the world, at great cost, to the wealthy few.

There was an old musketeer called Girardot, turned gardener, who specialised in peaches, lavishing on the fruit all the concentrated devotion he had previously given on the battlefield. He supplied peaches at court for Louis XIV and described the perfect peach, a description which is still poetically apt today:
'The skin should be glowingly yellow without a taint of green, it should come away easily from the flesh, it should always be cut with a knife so that not a drop of the delicious juice is lost and the flesh of the ideal peach melts as soon as

it is in the mouth, for the flesh of the peach is really only solidified water which reduces itself to liquid water for fear lest it be rushed by the teeth'.

Here the white peaches come first, very delicate in texture and flavour, best eaten plain or served in the simplest ways; then the yellow ones follow. There are two types, the ones which come away easily from the stone and the flavoursome, but more difficult to handle, clingstones.

To Poach Peaches
1 cup sugar
1½ cups water
1 teaspoon vanilla essence
6 peaches

Heat sugar, water and vanilla in a pan until the sugar is dissolved. Either peel the peaches first or cook and then peel later while warm. Simmer them gently until just tender. Transfer to a bowl and if there is a great deal of syrup boil it down a little. Pour the juices over the peaches. Leave to cool and then keep refrigerated. The liquid can be flavoured with a little brandy if you wish.

Savoury Stuffed Peaches

Three yellow peaches (not clingstone). Peel these and then cut in half. Poach them in 1 cup water, with 1 tablespoon sugar added until just tender. Drain and leave aside.

Filling
30 g (1 oz) butter
1 small white onion, finely diced
1 small green pepper, finely diced
1 teaspoon curry powder
1 tablespoon plain flour
½ cup milk
1 teaspoon Worcestershire sauce
1 tablespoon tomato sauce
1 small tin crab meat 165 g (5¾ oz)
or
¾ cup diced chicken (cooked)

Melt the butter, sauté onion, and pepper until softened. Add curry powder and flour. Cook a minute. Add milk and stir until thickened. Season with Worcestershire sauce, tomato sauce and check for salt and pepper. Remove the membrane from the crab and fold in (or chicken).
You may find the peach doesn't have a large enough cavity for stuffing. Using a teaspoon remove a little of the flesh. Place the peach halves in patty cases so they won't fall over during cooking.
Fill the centre with the crab or chicken filling.

Topping
30 g (1 oz) butter
1 tablespoon blanched almonds chopped roughly
3 tablespoons breadcrumbs, made from stale bread

Melt the butter and toss the almonds until golden. Add to the breadcrumbs. Press a little of this on top of each peach half. Bake them in a moderate oven, 180-190°C (350-375°F), about 15 minutes or until heated through. Serve with a spoonful of rice underneath to balance them.
This is best as an entrée or first course. When cooking the peaches make sure they are just tender as during the heating in the oven they will soften slightly but aren't nice if too firm.

Peaches in Strawberry Cream

6 ripe, white peaches
2 tablespoons castor sugar
½ cup white wine

Peel the peaches, cut into slices. Place these in a bowl; add sugar and white wine. Refrigerate. They will keep about 4 hours without changing colour — too long and they start to turn brown.

Sauce
1 cup cream
3 tablespoons castor sugar
1 tablespoon brandy
1 teaspoon vanilla essence
1 punnet strawberries, hulled

Whip the cream until stiff. Add sugar, brandy and vanilla and whisk gently. Keep 6 whole strawberries aside for garnishing. Chop the remainder and then crush lightly with a fork. Fold into the cream. Chill.
To Assemble: Place some of the peach slices in a crystal dish or champagne glass. Top with the cream and then garnish with a whole strawberry. Be sure to serve this dessert very cold.

Jellied Peaches

It is surprising how the peaches are even more delicious than usual when set in this jelly. It is a lovely summer dessert especially after a rich dinner.

6 medium-sized fresh yellow peaches
2 cups water
¾ cup sugar
1 teaspoon vanilla
1 tablespoon gelatine
2 tablespoons water
1 tablespoon lemon juice
2 tablespoons brandy (optional)

Peel the peaches and cut in halves, remove stones. Heat water, sugar and vanilla and when boiling add the peaches. Cover and cook over low heat until quite tender. Soften gelatine in the cold water. Dissolve over hot water and add to peaches with lemon juice. Leave to cool. Add brandy when cold. Pour into individual dishes to set or 1 large glass dish. Can be kept several days. Serve very cold with cream.

Apricots

To Poach
500 g (1 lb) apricots
¼ cup sugar, although quantity depends on the ripeness of the apricots
¾ cup water
½ teaspoon vanilla essence

Cut the apricots in half and stone them. Heat sugar, water and vanilla until sugar is dissolved and add apricot halves. Poach them gently and don't let them become too soft. Remove fruit and if there is too much liquid boil it quickly until it is reduced slightly. Cool and then serve chilled.

Russian Apricot Pudding

500 g (1 lb) apricots
½ cup sugar, although this depends on the tartness of the apricots
1 teaspoon vanilla essence
1 cup water

Halve and stone the apricots. Place sugar, vanilla and water into a saucepan. Warm and then add apricots. Cook gently until tender but don't let them get too soft. Remove from the juice and place into a shallow, ovenproof dish (about 4 cup size). They can be cooked beforehand and then put in the dish and placed in the oven for a few minutes while the topping is made.

Topping
1 tablespoon flour
2 tablespoons sugar
2 eggs
1 teaspoon vanilla essence
1 cup sour cream

Place flour and sugar in a basin and mix. Add eggs, beat with vanilla essence and then gradually beat in cream. Pour over the top of the warm apricots. Bake in moderate oven, 180-190°C (350-375°F), for about 30 minutes or until just set and firm on top. This pudding is equally nice hot or cold.
It can be made using any type of stewed fruits or berries.

Apricot Torte

1 kg (2 lb) apricots
1 cup sugar, although quantity depends on tartness of apricots
1 cup water
1 teaspoon vanilla essence

Halve and stone fruit. Place sugar, water and vanilla in a saucepan and add fruit. Cook until soft. Drain slightly. Place in shallow, ovenproof dish (about 6 cup size.)

90 g (3 oz) ground almonds
2 tablespoons castor sugar
3 eggs, separated
¼ teaspoon almond essence
rind of 1 orange
3 tablespoons castor sugar

Mix almonds, sugar, egg yolks, almond essence and rind of orange in a basin. This will be a very stiff mixture. Beat the egg whites separately, when stiff add the extra 3 tablespoons castor sugar and beat well. Fold half of this into the almond mixture, then the remaining half. Spread over the apricots and bake in moderate oven, 180-190°C (350-375°F), until centre is puffy and golden. Serve hot or cold with cream.
This can also be made using cooked apples as a base. In this case the grated rind of 1 lemon can be substituted for the orange rind in the topping.

Apricot Almond Tart

Serves 8

Pastry
1 cup plain flour
pinch salt
1 tablespoon castor sugar
60 g (2 oz) butter, cut in tiny pieces
grated rind of 1 lemon
1 egg yolk

Sift flour and salt into a basin. Add castor sugar. Place butter, lemon rind and egg into the centre and gradually work in the flour until a mealy mixture. Knead lightly and if too sticky to handle chill for 30 minutes. Roll out and line a flan tin (size 20 cm 8 inch). Chill while preparing filling.

Filling
½ cup apricot jam
1 cup lightly sweetened apricots, sieved
60 g (2 oz) ground almonds
1 tablespoon lemon juice
2 egg whites
2 tablespoons castor sugar

Cover the base of the tart with jam. If the jam is lumpy sieve it. Mix the apricot pulp with the ground almonds and lemon juice. Beat the egg whites until stiff. Add sugar, beat again. Fold into apricot mixture. Pour into pastry case. Bake in moderate oven, 180-190°C (350-375°F), about 30 minutes or until filling is set. Serve warm or cold.

SOME OTHER SUMMER FRUITS

Bananas

By and large, the commercial bananas are a complex plant, about whose origins experts have argued for years. The huge broad banana leaves and myriad individual blossoms produce a fruit which is still reasonably priced here, yet somewhat neglected in the kitchen as far as being used for exciting and interesting dishes.

Baked Bananas in Honey and Wine Sauce

6 bananas cut in half (make sure they're not too ripe)
⅓ cup honey
30 g (1 oz) butter
½ cup dry white wine
grated rind of 1 orange
½ teaspoon cinnamon
⅓ cup rum

Peel bananas, cut in half, and place in a small shallow ovenproof dish in one layer. Pour honey over the top. Cut the butter into tiny pieces and dot over bananas. Add white wine, grated orange rind and cinnamon. Bake in a moderate oven, 180-190°C (350-375°F), about 12-15 minutes until bananas are soft without being too limp. Baste a couple of times with liquid.
Before serving warm the rum. Flame and pour over the top. Serve plain or with ice cream.

Exotic Baked Bananas

The idea for this dish came from one of the most famous of Central American banana desserts. In the tropics bananas are utilised in many exotic and interesting ways. This dessert is fairly rich so goes best after a light dinner.

6 small ripe bananas
60 g (2 oz) butter
1 tablespoon brown sugar
1 tablespoon lemon juice

Topping
125 g (4 oz) cream cheese
1 tablespoon white sugar
1 tablespoon brown sugar
rind of 1 lemon
2 teaspoons lemon juice
1 teaspoon cinnamon
1 tablespoon rum
½ cup cream

Halve the bananas; cut each one into 3 strips. Melt the butter and cook the bananas a few at a time until lightly softened. Transfer to an ovenproof dish. It is best to use one which fits the bananas in 2 layers. A dish which is too shallow and long will mean there may not be enough topping to go around. Sprinkle with brown sugar and lemon juice.
Topping: Beat the cream cheese until soft, with sugars, lemon rind and juice, cinnamon and rum. Spread this over the banana strips. Lastly pour over the cream.
It can be prepared about 3 hours beforehand. Bake in a moderate oven, 180-190°C (350-375°F), for about 15 minutes.
Serve hot or just warm. It can be served plain or with ice cream.

NOTE: Topping can be doubled if you wish, depending on the size of the dish used and also on personal taste.

Banana and Shrimp Savouries

These savouries are very exotic but delicious. The idea is based on an African savoury but altered slightly. The original was so hot it was difficult to breathe after eating it, much less talk!

250 g (8 oz) prawns
1 large or 2 medium-sized bananas
1 teaspoon lemon juice
½ teaspoon tabasco
salt and pepper
2 teaspoons finely chopped chives
½ teaspoon fresh grated ginger
or
1 small piece ginger in syrup (about the size of a walnut)
breadcrumbs (made from stale bread)
light vegetable oil

Shell prawns and chop or mince very finely. Mash banana and mix through with lemon juice, tabasco, salt, pepper, chives and ginger. Form into small balls with your hands. Dip these in breadcrumbs and leave to chill for about 30 minutes. They can be kept chilled 4-5 hours. Heat oil and fry the balls either in a deep frying pan or shallow pan and turn once until golden. Takes about 1 minute. Sprinkle with a little extra salt and pepper before serving.

Raspberry Nut Torte (see p. 59)

Pineapple Flambé

1 medium-sized pineapple
2 tablespoons castor sugar
½ cup maple syrup
¼ cup orange juice
1 teaspoon grated orange rind
3 tablespoons orange curacao
1 tablespoon brandy

Remove the top from the pineapple. Slice off the base, stand upright and cut down through the peel being sure to remove all the little 'eyes'. Cut into dice, removing core. Sprinkle with the castor sugar. Mix together maple syrup, orange juice and rind. Place the pineapple in a frying pan or chafing dish and heat a moment, tossing. Add maple syrup and orange mixture and cook a minute. When all is heated, warm the orange curacao and brandy together in a small pan. Light and pour flaming over the top. Serve plain or with a side dish of ice cream. If put in the same bowl, the hot pineapple tends to curdle the ice cream.
The same dish is also delicious cooked and then served chilled.

Pineapple Alexandra

This is a classic dessert and although the ingredients are basically simple it is cleverly contrived to give an illusion of a spectacular masterpiece.

1 large ripe pineapple
2 punnets small strawberries
4 tablespoons castor sugar
2 tablespoons brandy
2 tablespoons kirsch

Remove top and base of pineapple. Hold upright and cut down through the peel using a sharp knife. Be sure to cut so that all the little 'eyes' are removed. Then cut into thin even slices.
Choose about 10 of the best slices and cut in half. Remove cores carefully and arrange on a flat plate. This should give you 20 even half pieces. Sprinkle the top with 2 tablespoons castor sugar, 1 tablespoon brandy and 1 tablespoon kirsch. Leave to stand at least 1 hour although they can be left for most of the day to marinate. Gather up the rest of the pineapple slices and scraps except the cores, and chop into dice. Place in a large bowl; sprinkle with 2 tablespoons castor sugar, 1 tablespoon brandy and 1 tablespoon kirsch. Stand aside for at least 1 hour.
Carefully wash the strawberries (or brush them with a pastry brush) and dry on kitchen paper. Keep some aside to garnish the dish (about 12 are needed altogether and add the rest to the chopped pineapple in the bowl. Keep the mixture chilled until ready to assemble the sweet, but don't keep too long or the strawberries will become soft.

Apricot Sauce
¾ cup apricot jam
1 tablespoon lemon juice

In a small saucepan simmer together the jam and lemon juice. Pour through a fine sieve and rub it through using the back of a spoon. It will thicken a little as it cools; if it becomes too thick, thin down with a little of the brandy and kirsch juices.

Cream filling
1 cup cream
2 tablespoons icing sugar
few drops vanilla essence

Beat the cream until slightly stiffened. Add the icing sugar and vanilla essence. Gently whisk until very stiff and keep refrigerated.

Scallops Ravigote (see p. 39)

65

To Assemble: To present this dessert most effectively use a large round platter with a slightly indented well in the centre, or else a platter with a slight edge to catch the juice. It can be assembled about 6 hours before eating, but must be kept refrigerated once it is put together.

First drain the pineapple pieces and strawberries and spoon into the centre of the serving dish. Pat into a small mount leaving a small gap between the fruit and the edge of the dish. Coat the fruit with some of the whipped cream, keeping back just a few spoonfuls to pipe over the top. Coat it evenly using a knife. This is quite easy to do. Lightly drain the slices of pineapple and arrange these around the mound, standing each one upright on one point and overlapping slightly. Press gently into the cream so they will stick. When you have finished the cream covered fruit should be completely ringed with pineapple and only the little bit of cream on top showing. Using a spoon, trickle the apricot sauce over the top of the pineapple, letting it drip down each slice until it is all thoroughly glazed. Pipe a large rosette in the centre of the sweet and place the best strawberry on top. Cut the remaining ones in half and arange around the base. Chill.

To Serve: Remove 2 pineapple slices and arrange in a ring. From the gap which is now left, spoon out some of the chopped fruit and cream and pile on top.

I must mention, it takes longer to read this than it takes to prepare the sweet.

Spiced Melon Balls

1 canteloupe or honey dew melon
½ cup red currant jelly
¾ cup orange juice
grated rind of 1 orange
1 teaspoon French mustard
2 tablespoons kirsch
seasoning of salt and pepper

Cut small balls from the canteloupe or honey dew melon and allow about 8 for each serving. The sauce is enough for about 48-50 melon balls. Melt the red currant jelly and add the orange juice, orange rind, mustard, kirsch and salt and pepper. Mix the sauce with the melon and chill for about an hour for flavour to mature. Serve very cold in small dishes. This is an appetizer rather than a dessert and has an interesting and spiced flavour. When melon is not in season, the same sauce can be poured over orange sections which have been cut out so no membrane is left (enough for 6 small oranges).

Canteloupe with Port

This is a ridiculously simple dish which is so good it is worth mentioning. The canteloupe needs to be perfectly ripe and at the peak of the season.

Choose 1 baby melon for each person and chill well. Cut a small piece from the top and remove the seeds using a spoon. Pour 1 tablespoon of port into each melon. Chill about another half an hour and then serve.

If you can only buy large melons, they need to be cut in halves and the port poured in the half. However, this is not quite so good as the delicious aroma that comes from the melon when guests lift the small lid.

Serve as a first course rather than as a dessert.

Passionfruit Syllabub

½ cup castor sugar
2 tablespoons lemon juice
3 tablespoons white wine
1 tablespoon brandy
8 passionfruit
1 cup cream

Mix together castor sugar, lemon juice, white wine, brandy and the strained juice of 5 of the passionfruit. (If all the pips go in it makes the syllabub too seedy.) Whip cream until very stiff and then gradually beat in the wine and passionfruit mixture. Lastly fold in the remaining pulp of 3 passionfruit. It should be fairly stiff. Chill but serve within 7 hours as it goes a bit wet. It will still taste delicious for a couple of days but doesn't look so nice.
Serve plain or with berry fruits and small biscuits.

Tropical Cream

4 egg yolks
4 tablespoons castor sugar
1 cup milk
grated rind of 1 orange
2 teaspoons gelatine and 1 tablespoon water
1 teaspoon vanilla
½ cup cream
6 passionfruit

Beat the egg yolks and sugar in a basin. Heat the milk with the orange rind. When hot, but not boiling, add to the egg yolks. Mix well and return to the saucepan. Cook, stirring continuously until slightly thickened. Do not let it boil. Soften gelatine in water and add to custard. Stir. Add vanilla and leave to cool. Whip the cream until stiff and fold through. Lastly stir in the pulp of the 6 passionfruit. Turn into a glass bowl or individual dishes or champagne glasses and chill.
This keeps well for several days.

Grape Ginger Cocktail

Serves 8

This is served very cold as a cocktail, however it would also be an excellent dessert after a rich dinner.

500 g (1 lb) Waltham Cross grapes
4 oranges
1 lemon
2 teaspoons castor sugar
½ teaspoon ground ginger (less if you like)
6 small pieces glacé ginger, or the ginger in syrup which can be bought in jars

Peel the grapes and remove seeds. Sorry about that but it is essential to the dish. It really only requires long fingernails and lots of patience.
Squeeze the orange and lemon juice. It should measure about ¾ cup. Mix into juice, sugar and ground ginger.
Slice the glacé or ginger in syrup into very tiny slithers and mix with juices. Pour over grapes and leave refrigerated for 24 hours before using.
Serve in champagne glasses, icy cold.
This should fill eight glasses, but depends on the size.

Paw Paw Mai Tai

1 small fresh paw paw or ½ large one
½ cup castor sugar
juice of 1 lemon
pulp of 3 passionfruit

Peel paw paw and remove seeds. Cut into neat dice. Sprinkle over the castor sugar and add lemon juice and passionfruit pulp. Stand at room temperature 1 hour for juices to collect and then chill. This is best served plain without cream and is a really refreshing dessert after a rich meal.

Plums in Port

500 g (1 lb) red plums
½ cup port
grated rind of 1 orange
juice of 1 orange
4 tablespoons red currant jelly
(sugar may be needed if the plums are very sour)

Halve the plums and stone them. Place port, orange rind and juice into a saucepan. Add the plums and cook gently until tender. Remove with a spoon. Add the red currant jelly to the juice and stir until it is dissolved. Pour this over the plums and leave to cool.
If you think it necessary add sugar to the port and orange rind when cooking the plums. Start with about ½ cup for sour plums. Remember too the red currant jelly will sweeten them slightly.

ICE CREAMS

The variety of flavourings, shapes and names are incredible, but then ice cream manufacturers will go to great lengths to create new and saleable flavours. Believed to have originated in China, ice cream travelled to Persia and then to Rome where frozen creams played a part in the lavish feasts. But it was the Italians who finally perfected them, elevating the dessert to grand heights. Really well-made ice cream from eggs and cream is a gorgeous luxury and easy to make. Ice creams made in the refrigerator without using an ice cream churn are perhaps not quite so smooth, but still have a good texture if you beat them again when they are firm. Once finished, they can be kept frozen well wrapped.

All the ice creams in this chapter are creamy and rich and can be kept successfully in the freezer of any refrigerator. Rather than being hard as a brick like the commercial ice cream, home-made should be rather creamy although still firm. The sugar content is very important. Too much and the ice cream becomes very soft; not enough and it has a rough and slightly icy texture.

Rich Milk Chocolate Ice Cream

2 eggs
2 tablespoons castor sugar
150 g (approx. 5 oz) milk chocolate
1 cup cream, lightly whipped

Place the eggs and sugar over a low heat, using a whisk; beat until warm and frothy (should only take about 2 minutes). Break the chocolate into pieces and place in basin or on a plate and melt over hot water. Add to the egg. Stir this chocolate mixture into the cream and then place in tin to freeze.

Almond Ice Cream

1 tablespoon finely chopped glacé cherries
1 tablespoon brandy
1 large egg
4 tablespoons castor sugar
2 tablespoons ground almonds
1 cup cream

Soak cherries in brandy. Place egg and sugar in a small pan. Beat with a whisk over low heat until frothy and warm. Don't overheat. Add almonds to dry frying pan and cook a moment until lightly coloured. Add to egg mixture. Add cherries and stir well. Beat cream until thick and fold in almond mixture. Line a log tin with foil as it's a bit hard to turn out. Pour in mixture and freeze. Stir this with a fork when it is partly frozen as the cherries have a tendency to sink to the bottom.

Chocolate Mousse Ice Cream

Serves 8

45 g (1½ oz) butter
185 g (6 oz) dark chocolate
3 large eggs
2 tablespoons castor sugar
½ cup cream, whipped until stiff

Melt the butter in a saucepan. Break the chocolate into pieces and add to the hot butter. Remove from the heat immediately and stir until chocolate is melted. If there isn't enough warmth for this return to the heat for a moment but be careful not to let it get too hot. Separate the eggs and add the egg yolks one at a time. The mixture should be smooth and glossy, if not warm slightly over a low heat. Beat the egg whites until stiff, add castor sugar and beat again. Fold the cream into this and lastly stir in chocolate mixture. Pour into tray and freeze. I like to make this in a metal steam pudding basin so it forms a round shape for cutting. It can be decorated when set with piped cream rosettes.

VARIATION: Make up the Chocolate Mousse Ice Cream as above and pour into basin shape. Before it is completely set use a spoon to make a hollow in the centre. Fill this hollow with Almond Cream and then leave to set. The combination of the very rich Chocolate Ice Cream and the light almond filling is delicious.

Almond Cream
½ cup cream, whipped until stiff
1 tablespoon icing sugar
4 crumbled almond macaroons
1 teaspoon vanilla essence
few drops almond essence

Fold icing sugar, macaroons, vanilla essence and almond essence into cream and use.

Banana Ice Cream

3 bananas, medium-sized to large
grated rind of 1 orange
¾ cup castor sugar
1 tablespoon brandy
1 cup cream, whipped

Mash the bananas well. Add the grated orange rind, castor sugar and brandy. Fold in the whipped cream. Freeze.

Apricot Ice Cream

185 g (6 oz) dried apricots
1 tablespoon lemon juice
1 cup cream
3 egg yolks
¾ cup castor sugar
2 tablespoons orange curaçao

Soak the apricots for 1 hour in water to just cover. Place in a pan, cook until tender; drain and sieve or put through *moulin*. Add 1 tablespoon lemon juice. Heat the cream. Beat the egg yolks and castor sugar until thick and lemon and add the hot cream. Return to the heat and cook until a thick custard, stirring continually. It doesn't take long but be careful not to let it boil. Mix in apricot purée and leave to cool. Add orange curaçao and freeze. When partly frozen remove and beat well. Refreeze.

This is beautiful if made in a pudding basin which has first been lined with the rich chocolate ice cream but made with dark chocolate, not milk. Freeze chocolate first until fairly firm, then spread in a layer around the basin. When the apricot ice cream has been beaten, fill into mould and freeze. Keep mould covered with foil. The combination of chocolate and apricot is really superb.

Brandied Fruit Ice Cream

Serves 10

Basic Ice Cream
3 large eggs
½ cup sugar
1 teaspoon vanilla
1 pint cream (2 cups)

Place the eggs, sugar and vanilla in a saucepan. Whisk over gentle heat until frothy. Be careful not to let this become too hot. It should really just be tepid at all times. Remove from the heat and leave to cool. Beat the cream until stiff. Fold the cooled egg mixture into the cream. Freeze in a large tin; a metal cake tin will do quite well.

Fruit Mixture
60 g (2 oz) butter
2 tablespoons brown sugar
1 peeled cooking apple, finely chopped
½ cup drained crushed pineapple
½ cup sultanas
2 tablespoons mixed peel, chopped
1 tablespoon chopped walnuts
½ teaspoon almond essence
grated rind of 1 orange
grated rind of 1 lemon
½ teaspoon cinnamon
½ teaspoon nutmeg
3 tablespoons brandy
2 tablespoons orange curaçao

Place all the above ingredients in a saucepan, except brandy and curaçao. Cook, covered, over gentle heat about 20 minutes or until apple is softened and it is a fairly thick mixture. Remove and cool slightly. Add brandy and curaçao. Remove basic ice cream from freezer and beat well until fluffy. Fold in fruit mince. Return to freezer until set. This keeps well although after a couple of weeks, it has a tendency to soften down as it is kept, owing to the natural sugar which comes out of the fruit. Serve cut in slices. It can also be made in a pudding basin tin for Christmas and decorated as an ice cream pudding.

Autumn

PANCAKES

In the England of old, the eve of Ash Wednesday, or the eve of Lent was a time of great feasting. On this Shrove Tuesday among other things, eggs, flour and dripping needed to be used up and pancakes were popular; the day eventually becoming known as Pancake Tuesday. It was the custom for children to go from door to door, asking for pancakes. Some were polite and well mannered about it, others turned the old custom into a roughhouse.

Since the time of Henry VIII, at eleven o'clock in the morning of Shrove Tuesday, the verger of Westminster College emerges from the kitchen followed by the cook. The cook carries a long handled skillet which contains one large pancake. The pair of them proceed to the bar which separates lower and upper schools at Westminster and fling the pancake into the group of students. They make a rush for it for the one coming back with the largest piece out of the mêlée gets a reward.

One of the cooks some years ago ruined that traditional ceremony by hurling the pancake high into the air where it lodged on a beam sixteen feet above the crowd and despite all efforts it could not be dislodged.

Most people enjoy pancakes all year round now. There have been vast improvements in the variety and texture as against the original pancakes. They are versatile and can be used as entrées, main dishes or desserts. The pancakes in this section are a little different to the style that John Taylor 'the water poet' gave an account of:

> 'There is a thing called wheaten floure, which the cookes do mingle with water, eggs, spices and other tragical, magical inchantments, put it little and little into a frying pan of boiling suet where it makes a confused, dismall hissing . . .'

Pancake Basic Mixture

¾ cup plain flour
pinch salt
1 egg and 1 egg yolk
¾ to 1 cup milk
1 tablespoon light vegetable oil
or
1 tablespoon melted butter

Sift the flour and salt into a bowl. Make a well in the centre and add the whole egg and egg yolk. Mix in a ¼ cup milk and gradually stir from the centre incorporating the flour. Then gradually add enough milk until it is the consistency of cream. Lastly, add vegetable oil or butter. If not absolutely smooth strain through a fine sieve. Leave to stand for 1 hour or longer. If it thickens up too much, add a little extra milk.

The perfect crêpes should be (hopefully) paper-thin, tender and delicately brown — almost on the transparent side. An ideal crêpe pan is about 12 cm (5 inch across, heavy on the base and if it has sloping sides so much the better. The above quantity of batter makes about 18 crêpes.

Heat the pan first, then place in a small piece of butter. Ladle just enough batter to cover the base in a very thin layer. The pan should be hot enough so that it sets immediately. Cook over a fairly high heat until the rim shows slightly brown; turn it with a spatula and cook only very briefly on the other side. This side will be speckled rather than brown and is classified as the wrong side of the crêpe. Slide out onto a plate and continue, using a tiny piece of butter each time. Pile them up on top of each other, they won't stick together and cover with foil if not using for a little while.

Butter Crêpes

½ cup plain flour
pinch salt
1 teaspoon sugar
1 egg
1 egg yolk
½ cup milk
60 g (2 oz) butter

Sift the flour and salt into a basin. Add the sugar. Make a well in the centre and break in the egg. Add the yolk and a tablespoon of milk. Stir gradually with a fork, working the flour down into the centre. Melt the butter. Leave to cool. Add butter with enough milk to make it the consistency of cream. Leave to stand for 1 hour or longer and if it goes too thick, add extra milk. Make up in a crêpe pan as usual.

These are light but have a delicious butter taste and go well sprinkled with lemon and sugar.

Makes 12 crêpes about 12 cm (5 inch) in size.

Orange Crêpes

First make up 12 crêpes.

Orange Butter
90 g (3 oz) unsalted butter
rind of 1 large orange
3 tablespoons icing sugar

Cream butter, with orange rind and sugar until fluffy. Spread a thin layer on each crêpe. Fold in triangles and leave aside. These can be prepared several hours beforehand and kept covered.

Orange Sauce
30 g (1 oz) butter
4 tablespoons castor sugar
¾ cup orange juice
1 tablespoon lemon juice
1 tablespoon brandy
3 tablespoons orange flavoured liqueur

Melt the butter and add sugar. Stir until mixture is foaming but don't let the sugar brown and turn to toffee. Add orange juice, lemon juice and cook gently until all the sugar bits are quite dissolved. This part can be done beforehand and then the sauce can be reheated.

Place crêpes in sauce and warm gently. Lastly add brandy and orange flavoured liqueur; heat through and serve.

Lemon Crêpes with Strawberry Sauce

First make up 18 crêpes using Basic Crêpe Mixture.

Lemon Butter
60 g (2 oz) butter
grated rind of 1 lemon
2 tablespoons icing sugar

Mash butter and lemon rind together and mix in icing sugar. Place the crêpes, folded in quarters in an ovenproof dish just slightly overlapping. Dot the top of them with tiny pieces of the lemon butter. Bake in a moderate oven, 180-190°C (350-375°F), for about 8 minutes or until heated through and the butter is foaming.
Serve with Strawberry Sauce.
They can be prepared in the morning successfully as long as the ovenproof dish is tightly covered.

Strawberry Sauce
45 g (1½ oz) butter
3 tablespoons castor sugar
¼ cup lemon juice
2 tablespoons brandy
1 tablespoon orange flavoured liqueur
1 punnet sliced strawberries

Melt butter; add sugar; stir until foaming; don't brown; add lemon, brandy and liqueur. Add strawberries last and warm through but don't overcook or they become rather acidic.

Pumpkin Pancakes

Makes about 12 pancakes.
This may sound strange but they are light and very delicate in flavour and make an interesting side dish served with chicken or meats.

500 g (1 lb) pumpkin (Use a dry baking variety such as a butternut or a blue pumpkin)
2 tablespoons plain flour
¼ teaspoon salt
little pepper
¼ teaspoon nutmeg
pinch cayenne
1 large egg

Cook pumpkin in salted water. Drain well and sieve or mash. Beat flour, salt, pepper, nutmeg, cayenne and egg into pumpkin purée.

To Cook
30 g (1 oz) butter
1 tablespoon oil

Heat the butter and oil. Place a tablespoon of the mixture in the pan and cook, turning once, until golden and firm. They can be kept warm in the oven, covered loosely with foil until all are cooked.

Spinach Pancakes

1 cup plain flour
1 teaspoon salt
½ teaspoon nutmeg
pinch sugar
pinch cayenne pepper
2 large eggs
1 cup milk
1 cup cooked spinach, well drained and chopped
(If you wish 1 cup cooked frozen spinach in place of fresh can be used. A 280 g (9 oz) packet of frozen spinach makes a 1 cup quantity when drained)

Sift flour into a bowl with salt. Add nutmeg, sugar, cayenne and eggs to the centre. Gradually stir from the centre incorporating the flour as you go. Add milk until a smooth batter. Lastly stir in the spinach. Leave to stand for 1 hour.

To Make Up
butter
1 cup finely diced ham

Heat a pan and melt a knob of butter. Place in 1 tablespoon of the spinach batter and cook until brown on one side, sprinkle the uncooked side with a little of the finely chopped ham and turn. Cook until the other side is golden. They can be kept warm in a low oven loosely covered with foil.
Serve with the side up that is covered with the little crispy bits of ham.
Can be served as a vegetable course or a light luncheon dish accompanied by Ligonberries. (These can be bought in tins or jars in gourmet food shops. They are a small tart berry usually imported from Scandinavia.)

Stuffed Crêpes à la Maison

Make up 12 crêpes using basic method.

Filling
30 g (1 oz) butter
3 large mushrooms, chopped finely
little salt and pepper
2 hard boiled eggs
1 cup cooked spinach, well drained (use either fresh or 1 frozen packet (280 g or 9 oz) will cook up to 1 cup)
2 slices ham, cut small

Melt the butter and cook diced mushroom with a little salt and pepper. Mash the hard boiled eggs, add mushroom and then the drained spinach and diced ham.
Make up the sauce and mix 3 tablespoons of this into the filling. Keep the remainder of sauce aside for later.

Sauce
45 g (1½ oz) butter
1 tablespoon plain flour
1 cup milk
salt and pepper
½ teaspoon dry, English-style mustard
60 g (2 oz) finely diced gruyère cheese
¼ cup cream

Melt the butter, add flour and cook until foaming. Add milk, salt, pepper and mustard and cook, stirring constantly until thickened. Simmer for 5 minutes. Remove from the heat and add cheese. Stir until cheese is melted. Lastly add cream. Place a bare 2 tablespoons filling on each crêpe. Roll up tucking in the ends and place in a buttered, shallow, ovenproof dish. Spoon a little of the remaining sauce over the top of each crêpe. If the sauce has become too thick to spoon, warm gently.

To Finish
2 tablespoons grated, tasty cheese

Sprinkle cheese over the top and reheat in moderate oven, 180-190°C (350-375°F), for about 15 minutes.
They can be made 12 hours before serving and kept covered in the refrigerator.

MUSHROOMS

The Egyptians who believed that mushrooms grew up like magic overnight, permitted only the Pharaohs to eat them; they were considered too special for the ordinary people. To know them, to hunt for them, to eat them cooked or sometimes uncooked, and always the chance in your ignorance to be poisoned by them, that is one of the factors that have deterred many would be mushroomers.

It was in France that the cultivated mushroom first started during the 1700s and they were grown in the abandoned caves around Paris.

It may be worth noting that the inedible mushrooms are not able to grow alongside the modern cultivated ones because they cannot thrive under the conditions necessary for the cultivated variety. The cultivated mushrooms are oyster white, or of the brown variety with smooth and unblemished caps. As they mature the moisture evaporates and the cap will open; the older ones turn darker after cooking and should be used quickly. The size of the cap has nothing to do with quality; the best to buy depends on what you intend to use them for. The stems also are edible but can be fibrous. Try to find short stemmed mushrooms, or if the stalk looks a bit tough remove it. Don't wash them as the caps absorb water like a sponge. During cooking this water cooks out into the pan making quite a difference to the flavour. Don't peel them either as the skin contains most of the flavour and adds to the texture. If you feel they have been handled carelessly wipe them clean with damp kitchen paper, although this is really a rather unnecessary chore.

Australian field mushrooms are found during autumn and need to be handled quite differently, probably one of the best things about them is the fun of the hunt. They need to be quickly washed and usually are best peeled because of the dubious thoughts as to who, or what, has been around the paddocks. They have a rich flavour, cook up darker in colour and in particular are excellent in soups and casserole-type dishes.

One of the greatest of all mushroom preparations, *duxelles,* was created in the eighteenth century by a French chef. This is a mixture of finely minced, or chopped mushrooms combined with shallot or onion and gently cooked in a little butter until quite dry.

It has an intense mushroom flavour and can be refrigerated for 1 week. It is invaluable for mixing into stuffings or sauces and can also be mixed with cream, heated and served as a sauce with various meat dishes.

Marinated Mushrooms	**750 g (1½ lb) small button mushrooms**

Marinated Mushrooms

Serves 8

750 g (1½ lb) small button mushrooms
1½ cups water
2 teaspoons salt
½ cup white vinegar
1 small bay leaf
1 medium-sized white onion

Cut the stalks of the mushrooms level with the caps. Place in a saucepan with the water. Bring to the boil and cook for 2 minutes. Drain but keep the liquid. Place back in the saucepan ¾ cup of this mushroom liquid, the salt, vinegar and bay leaf. Bring to the boil. Cut the white onion into wafer thin circles. Layer the mushrooms in a glass container with the onion circles. Pour over the hot liquid. Leave to stand for 24 hours before serving.

Serve with small toothpicks through the centre of each one as a savoury or they are also delicious as an hors d'oeuvres.

They can be kept refrigerated for 1 week.

Mushrooms in White Wine

500 g (1 lb) small button mushrooms
60 g (2 oz) butter
1 large white onion, cut in thin rings
1 cup dry white wine
pinch dried rosemary or a couple of fresh sprigs
salt and pepper
2 tablespoons cream
1 tablespoon finely chopped parsley

Remove stalks from mushrooms and cut them in thick slices.

Melt 30 g (1 oz) of the butter, add mushrooms and cook about 2 minutes or until just barely softened. Remove. Melt remaining 30 g (1 oz) butter and add onion. Sauté a couple of minutes, pour in white wine, add salt, pepper and rosemary and simmer until onions are quite tender. Return mushrooms to the pan and heat through. Add cream and parsley and serve accompanied by garlic toast.

Garlic Toast
60 g (2 oz) butter
1 tablespoon finely chopped parsley
1 large clove crushed garlic
pinch cayenne pepper

Mash butter with parsley, garlic and pepper. Spread this on freshly made toast. It makes enough for 6 slices. It can either be eaten with the mushroom, or they can be spooned over it.

Baby Crumbed Mushrooms

18 small button mushrooms
salt and pepper
plain flour, seasoned
1 large egg and 1 tablespoon oil and 1 tablespoon water
breadcrumbs made from stale bread
2 tablespoons oil
30 g (1 oz) butter

Remove the mushroom stalks. Season caps well. Dip in flour. Mix egg with oil and water and beat. Dip mushrooms in this and then lastly coat with breadcrumbs. Chill. Heat the oil and butter; when foaming add the mushrooms and fry turning so both sides are cooked until they are golden in colour and slightly softened. Serve piping hot with savoury mayonnaise.

Savoury Mayonnaise
¼ cup mayonnaise
¼ cup sour cream
3 slices sour cucumber, chopped finely
1 teaspoon capers, chopped finely
1 tablespoon parsley, finely chopped

Mix all the ingredients, check for seasoning and keep cold. The mushroom caps can be filled with a little of this sauce before eating.

Savoury Stuffed Mushrooms

30 g (1 oz) butter
1 white onion, finely diced
12 medium-sized to large mushrooms (choose the button-shaped ones rather than flat, otherwise the filling tends to fall off)
salt and pepper
250 g (½ lb) prawns, peeled and cut in small pieces
or
¾ cup finely diced, cooked chicken

Melt the butter and cook the onion until soft. Place in basin and mix with prawns or chicken. Remove the stalks from the mushrooms, season the caps with salt and pepper and fill with prawn or chicken mixture.

Sauce
30 g (1 oz) butter
1 tablespoon plain flour
1 cup milk
pinch mustard, salt and pepper

Melt the butter, add the flour and cook until foaming. Add milk, mustard, pepper and salt and stir until thickened and boiling. Turn down the heat and simmer for 5 minutes. Coat the top of each stuffed mushroom with the sauce. Then sprinkle over a teaspoon of the topping.

Topping
1 cup breadcrumbs
2 tablespoons grated cheese
45 g (1½ oz) butter
1 clove garlic, crushed

Mix the crumbs and cheese in a bowl. Melt the butter and add the garlic to this. Stir into the breadcrumbs. These mushrooms can be stuffed beforehand and kept covered in the refrigerator for 6 hours.
To Cook: Place the mushrooms on a well buttered tray. Bake in a moderate oven, 180-190°C (350-375°F), for 12 to 15 minutes.

Savoury Mushroom Soufflé

12 tiny button mushrooms
30 g (1 oz) butter
1 small white onion, diced finely
1 small green pepper, diced finely
¼ cup finely diced ham
2 tablespoons grated tasty cheese
1 teaspoon Worcestershire sauce
1 egg separated
seasoning of salt and pepper

Remove stalks from mushrooms. Cut stalks up very finely. Melt butter, add stalks, onion, pepper and cook until softened. Remove to a basin and mix with ham, cheese, Worcestershire sauce and yolk of the egg. Season well with salt and pepper. Close to serving time, beat the egg white until stiff and fold into the mixture. Season the mushroom caps with salt and pepper and cover with mixture. Bake in shallow, greased, ovenproof dish in moderate oven, 180-190°C (350-375°F), for 12 minutes or until the top is puffed and golden.
Serve as an appetizer.

Mushrooms in a Bag

This is not such a strange dish as it may sound. The bag in reality is a crêpe which enfolds a mushroom filling. A most unusual and attractive dish — in flavour and presentation — and although it takes a little time, it can be prepared well beforehand.

Make up 6 large crêpes (25 cm or 10 inch) using the basic crêpe mixture.

Filling
9 medium-sized mushrooms
60 g (2 oz) butter
1 medium-sized white onion, finely diced
2 rashers bacon, chopped finely
salt and pepper
1 tablespoon cream

To Finish
½ cup finely diced or grated gruyère
30 g (1 oz) butter

Remove the stalks from the mushrooms. Melt 30 g (1 oz) of butter and sauté 6 only of the mushroom caps for a minute until slightly softened. Put aside. Dice stalks finely and also cut up the remaining 3 mushrooms into thin slices. Melt the other 30 g (1 oz) of butter, add the onion, bacon, mushroom pieces and sauté until softened, seasoning with salt and pepper. Lastly, add the cream and leave aside to cool slightly. Place a teaspoon of the filling on each crêpe; top with a whole mushroom and then the remaining filling divided between them. Cut some long, thin strips of foil and fold over to form a double thickness, about the size of string. Use this like a tie to hold the top of the crêpe so it forms a little sack. This may sound difficult but is quite easy to do. Sprinkle the top of the crêpes with gruyère. Melt the butter and trickle this over the top. Place them gently in a buttered, shallow, ovenproof dish. They can be kept like this for 12 hours. Bake in a moderate oven, 180-190°C (350-375°F), for 10 to 12 minutes.
Serve with Tomato Wine Sauce.

Tomato Wine Sauce
60 g (2 oz) butter
1 small white onion, finely diced
1 large ripe tomato, cut in rough pieces
1 teaspoon sugar
salt and pepper
½ cup white wine

Melt butter, cook onion until softened, add tomato, seasonings and wine, and simmer until tomato is cooked. Sieve or put through *moulin*. Keep aside. Can be made and kept refrigerated for 24 hours.

Basic Sauce
60 g (2 oz) butter
1 tablespoon plain flour
1 cup milk

Melt butter, add flour and cook until foaming; then add milk and stir constantly until boiling. Cook a couple of minutes. Mix the tomato and wine sauce into this; check for seasoning and keep warm.
This is served in a sauceboat with the Mushrooms in a Bag. It can be made beforehand and kept warm by standing in a basin over hot water or in a double boiler.

FISH AND SHELLFISH

There are seventy-two varieties of fish listed as commercial by the Fisheries Department. However, in fish shops the choice seems to be limited to about six types. The public are extremely conservative and obviously until they are willing to experiment and become more adventurous the marketing of fish will remain restricted. Not that there is anything wrong with these varieties, but it seems astounding in a country which is filled with such a diversity of fish and crustaceans in the seas and rivers that such ignorance and lack of basic information abounds as to the preparation and cooking.

First catch your fish of course. Regardless of what variety it is, a self-caught fish always seems to taste delicious. If this is not possible select from the best fish shop or fish market near by.

Many people find frozen fish convenient and tasty. I don't. Unless I can get really fresh fish I don't bother serving it. If you do use frozen fish however, remove from the deep freeze at least 24 hours before using and leave to defrost at the bottom of the refrigerator. Never soak it and once thawed, don't refreeze.

When buying fish the eyes should be clear and bright — not dull — the scales moist — not slimy — the flesh firm and springy and the gills a clear, bright red. If sold in fillets they should be firm and white in appearance, fillets which have a yellow or creamy look should be rejected.

Cook your fish just long enough so the translucence changes to opaque white as overcooking coarsens the flesh.

Baked Fish Fillets with Tomato and Caper Sauce

6 small fillets of fish, whiting or bream are excellent cooked this way. Otherwise any small fresh fillets will do.

Sauce
2 tablespoons vegetable oil
1 large white onion, finely diced
1 clove garlic, crushed
500 g (1 lb) ripe tomatoes, peeled, cut in small pieces
½ teaspoon dry English-style mustard
½ teaspoon salt
black pepper
½ teaspoon sugar
2 teaspoons chopped capers
2 teaspoons tomato paste

Wash and dry the fish; check and remove any small bones that may have been left in. Heat the oil, add onion and garlic, and sauté until they are softened. Add tomatoes, mustard, salt, pepper, sugar, capers and tomato paste. Simmer gently about 15 minutes or until lightly thickened. This can be made beforehand and kept refrigerated and can be kept for several days. If the sauce tastes too acidic, add a little more sugar.

6 thin slices lemon
buttered shallow ovenproof dish

Place the fish in the ovenproof dish, pour over the sauce and place 1 slice of lemon on each fish fillet. Cover the dish with a piece of foil. Bake in moderate oven, 180-190°C (350-375°F), until tender. The time depends entirely on the size of the fish fillets.
This makes enough for an entrée; double if you wish to serve it as a main dinner.

Whole Fish Stuffed with Egg and Anchovy (see p. 83)

Fish Fillets with Prawn Stuffing

12 small fillets of fine textured fish, such as whiting fillets about 60 to 90 g (2 to 3 oz) are a good size for this dish
Lemon juice
60 g (2 oz) butter
1 large white onion, finely diced
½ teaspoon curry powder
1 tablespoon plain flour
1 cup milk
¼ teaspoon salt
250 g (8 oz) prawns, shelled and deveined)
1 teaspoon Worcestershire sauce
3 tablespoons breadcrumbs

Have the fish filleted and check to see that the small bones near the top are also removed. If not, pull them out with the point of a knife and your fingers. Squeeze a little lemon juice over the fish. Melt butter, sauté onion until softened. Add curry; let fry ½ minute; add plain flour and cook until foaming. Add milk; stir until the sauce is thickened, seasoning with salt and Worcestershire sauce. Remove from heat; mix in prawns, chopped up into tiny pieces. Leave to cool slightly and stir in breadcrumbs. This mixture needs to be quite thick or it will not stay in between the fish. If it isn't thick, add another spoonful of breadcrumbs. Place 6 fish fillets in a shallow, greased ovenproof dish. Top with the filling, dividing it evenly between the 6. Then press another fillet on top of each one making a type of sandwich.

Tomato Topping for Fish
30 g (1 oz) butter
1 large ripe tomato, peeled
little salt and pepper
1 teaspoon brown sugar
1 teaspoon Worcestershire sauce

Melt butter. Cut tomato into small pieces and add. Season with salt, pepper, brown sugar and Worcestershire sauce. Cook a couple of minutes until a lightly thickened sauce. Spoon a little of this on top of the fish. Bake in a moderate oven, 180-190°C (350-375°F), about 20 minutes or until the fish is tender. Be careful not to overcook it.
This is a delicious entrée or main course and simple because there is not the last minute work and cooking that is usually associated with all fish dishes. For a main dinner you can buy slightly larger fillets of whiting and make 1½ times the filling and topping.

Whiting Adele

6 fillets of whiting
plain flour, seasoned with a little salt and pepper
1 large egg, beaten
1 tablespoon oil
30 g (1 oz) butter

Dip the whiting in the plain flour and then in the egg. Heat oil and butter in a frying pan and when very hot, add whiting. Cook until golden on both sides. They should only take a couple of minutes. Don't overcook or this fish goes dry.
While the fish is cooking prepare the sauce. It only takes a couple of minutes.

Sauce
30 g (1 oz) butter
45 g (1½ oz) pine nuts
1 small cooking apple, peeled and cut in small dice
1 small banana, sliced thinly
little salt and pepper
pinch sugar
2 teaspoons lemon juice
1 tablespoon mayonnaise

Melt the butter in a small saucepan. Add the nuts and apple and cook until nuts are golden and apple is tender. This only takes a minute or so. Add banana and cook 30 seconds more. Don't overcook or the banana goes too mushy. Season with salt, pepper and sugar. Remove from the heat; add lemon juice and mayonnaise. Stir and spoon immediately over the fish. Serves 6 as an entrée. Double the quantities if serving as a main dinner.

Stuffed Flounder Fillets

3 large flounders

Remove the fillets from either side and the dark skin. Place the bones that are left in a saucepan. Add a little water just to cover, salt, a slice of onion and cook covered to make just a little fish stock. Strain and keep this refrigerated.

Filling
220 g (7 oz) tinned salmon
¼ teaspoon salt
pepper
1 teaspoon lemon juice
1 tablespoon cream
1 egg white, stiffly beaten

Drain liquid from salmon. Mash well, adding salt and pepper, lemon and cream. Fold in the egg white. The mixture should be fairly stiff. Place a little in the centre of each fish fillet and roll up. Pack them together fairly tightly so they won't unroll during cooking in a shallow ovenproof dish. The size depends a little on the thickness of the flounder.

To Cook
½ cup fish stock
2 tablespoons white wine

Pour this stock and wine over fish. Cover the top with a piece of buttered foil and bake in a moderate oven, 180-190°C (350-375°F), for about 25 minutes or until the fish is tender. Remove fillets.

Sauce
60 g (2 oz) butter
1 tablespoon lemon juice
1 cup small sultana grapes
(or larger grapes can be used but they need to be cut in half and seeded and peeled)

Melt butter; add lemon and grapes. Cook quickly a couple of minutes and serve over fish fillets.

Whole Fish stuffed with Egg and Anchovy

6 small bream (or any firm, fresh, small fish will do)
salt and pepper

Stuffing
60 g (2 oz) butter
1 white onion, finely diced
1 clove garlic, crushed
4 medium-sized mushrooms, stalks removed, diced finely
3 hard boiled eggs
1 tin anchovies (45 g, 1½ oz)
1 cup breadcrumbs
pepper
4 tablespoons finely chopped parsley
1 large egg
1 teaspoon lemon juice

Scale and clean the fish. Cut 2 slashes with a sharp knife through the thickest part. Season outside with salt and pepper. Make up the stuffing: melt the butter, add the onion, garlic and mushrooms and cook gently until softened. Mash the eggs in a bowl and add the onion mixture with anchovies, breadcrumbs, pepper and parsley. Bind with the egg and lemon juice. Fill this stuffing into the fish, dividing evenly between the 6. It is not necessary to tie or sew them as when wrapped in the foil package, the stuffing stays in quite well.

To Cook the Fish
45 g (1½ oz) butter
6 squares foil
12 thin slices lemon

Melt the butter and brush the foil. Place 1 slice lemon on the foil and place 1 fish on this; then another slice of lemon. Wrap up in foil. Place on a tray and bake in a moderate oven, 180-190°C (350-375°F), until tender. This depends on the size of the fish. A bream about 250 g (8 oz) will take approximately 20-25 minutes. Remove the foil package and serve each one with a little extra butter melted over the top.

Prawns in Curry Cream Sauce

Serves 4 as an entrée

500 g (1 lb) prawns
60 g (2 oz) butter
1 white onion, finely diced
½ teaspoon curry powder
2 tablespoons brandy
½ cup cream
salt and pepper

Shell and devein prawns. Melt butter, add onion and cook until soft; add curry and prawns and toss until warmed through. Pour over brandy and light. Add cream, salt and pepper. Cook a moment until prawns are heated and sauce is lightly thickened. Do not overcook or prawns will toughen. Although this dish has curry, it is a very small amount so the flavour of the prawns is still prominent. It can be adjusted if you would prefer a stronger curry flavour.

Seafood Aurore

250 g (½ lb) scallops
1 cup water
½ cup wine
little salt
500 g (1 lb) prawns

Separate the coral from the white part of the scallop and clean. Bring the water and wine to the boil with salt. Add white part of scallop, cook 3 minutes, and then add coral and cook 2 minutes. Drain. Keep liquid and cut white into slices if large. Shell and devein prawns and cut into 2 or 3 pieces if large.

Tomato Mixture
30 g (1 oz) butter
1 small bunch spring onions, chopped roughly
3 ripe tomatoes, peeled, chopped in pieces
½ teaspoon salt
little black pepper
1 teaspoon sugar

Melt the butter, add the onion and cook a couple of minutes until slightly softened. Add tomatoes, salt, pepper and sugar and cook until the tomatoes are quite soft.

White Sauce
30 g (1 oz) butter
2 tablespoons plain flour
¾ cup milk
½ cup liquid from the scallops

Melt butter, add the flour and cook a moment until the flour is foaming. Add milk and liquid from the scallops. Cook, stirring occasionally until thickened. Add the tomato mixture to this and stir together. Lastly fold in the seafood and check for seasoning. This dish can be made beforehand and successfully reheated provided it is not overcooked or the seafood will toughen.
Serve either with little pastry crescents or some plain rice. This is a very delicate dish in flavour and appearance.
A little finely chopped parsley can be used if you wish, for decoration.

Crayfish Puff with Fresh Chutney

This dish can be made using crayfish, or if you are lucky enough to be able to get some fresh crab, or else prawns. It is also excellent made with cooked chicken instead of shellfish for a change.

1 cup milk
1 sliced onion and a little nutmeg
salt and pepper
60 g (2 oz) butter
1 tablespoon plain flour
½ teaspoon curry powder
1 cup crayfish, cut into cubes
3 large hard boiled eggs, chopped roughly
500 g (1 lb) puff pastry
1 egg for glazing

Heat the milk with onion and seasonings. Leave to stand half an hour and strain. Melt the butter; add flour and curry and cook 1 minute. Pour in milk; bring to the boil, stirring continuously. Add crayfish (crab, prawns or chicken), with roughly chopped eggs. Mix together gently and spread out to cool on a plate.
Roll out puff pastry thinly and cut out 2 circles each about the size of a large dinner plate. Spread the cooled filling on this leaving a small edge. Brush this edge with egg and then cover with the other circle. Pinch pleat the edges all the way around and brush these with egg and then brush over the top. Prick in the centre. Chilled it looks a bit like a hat at this stage but when cooked puffs up to a larger golden circle.
Can be kept 24 hours at this stage.
Bake in moderately hot oven, 180-190°C (350-375°F), for 25 minutes.
Serve cut in slices with fresh chutney. Serves 4 as a luncheon dish; 6-8 as an entrée.

Fresh Chutney for Crayfish Puff
1 small apple
1 small white onion
1 large ripe tomato, skinned
1 small stalk celery
1 small pepper
1 small clove garlic, crushed
1 teaspoon mint, finely chopped
2 teaspoons horseradish relish
2 teaspoons sugar
1 tablespoon white vinegar

Peel apple and grate it into a saucepan. Chop onion, tomato, celery and pepper finely and add with garlic. Cook gently until just boiling. Simmer for about 1 minute; add mint, horseradish, sugar and vinegar. Leave to cool. Serve cold with the crayfish puff. It keeps well for several days in the refrigerator.

Oysters in Champagne

This is really extravagant but quite a gorgeous dish.

3 dozen oysters
1 cup champagne
4 egg yolks
2 tablespoons cream
a little salt and pepper

Pour the champagne into a shallow pan. Remove oysters from the shells. When the champagne is bubbling add oysters. Simmer for 30 seconds. Remove and return to the shells. Beat egg yolks, cream and salt and pepper in a basin. Tip the hot champagne into this, return to the pan. Stir until it thickens but don't let it boil.
Cover each oyster with a spoonful of sauce. Arrange them on a tray of rock salt so they will balance. This can all be done a little time before serving.
When serving, preheat griller, grill until the sauce on top is golden and the oysters heated through but don't overcook.
Eat them with the remainder of the champagne.

SOME OTHER DISHES FOR LENT

And for those who sometimes like meatless meals during Lent or Easter, but are not able to always obtain fresh fish, here are a few other interesting dishes to try.

Eggs en cocotte

6 small ramekins or *cocottes* are used for this dish which makes a luxurious breakfast or light lunch.

60 g (2 oz) butter
12 spring onions, roughly chopped
125 g (¼ lb) mushrooms, sliced thinly
½ cup diced ham
6 (or 12) eggs, this is according to appetite
a little salt and pepper
6 tablespoons cream

Brush the inside of the ramekins or *cocottes* with a little butter.
Melt the butter; sauté spring onions a moment; add mushrooms and cook until softened, seasoning with salt and pepper. Remove and mix with ham.
Spoon this mixture into the base of the dishes. Break one (or two) eggs over the top, season and spoon 1 tablespoon cream over the egg.
Place in a shallow pan of boiling water; cover the top loosely with a sheet of foil. Cook in moderate oven, 180-190°C (350-375°F), until the eggs are just set on top (approx. 12 to 15 minutes). Don't overcook or they are spoilt. Serve with buttered triangles of toast.

Luxury Scrambled Eggs

6 eggs
1 tablespoons white wine
3 tablespoons cream
black pepper (no salt)
125 g (¼ lb) smoked salmon
60 g (2 oz) butter
1 large white onion, finely diced
1 green pepper, finely diced
1 jar caviar about 60 g (2 oz)

Beat eggs, wine and cream with pepper. Dice smoked salmon and add. As this is usually quite salty, leave until the finish before adding any extra seasoning. Melt butter, cook onion and green pepper until softened. Pour in eggs, stir over the heat until just barely setting. Snatch from the heat before they go too firm. Serve with fingers of toast.
Put the caviar in a small bowl on the table and each guest spoons a little over the top of the eggs.

Mushroom Stuffed Eggs

6 hardboiled eggs
30 g (1 oz) butter
1 small white onion, finely chopped
125 g (4 oz) finely chopped mushrooms
2 tablespoons white wine
little salt and pepper
2 teaspoons mayonnaise
1 tablespoon cream

Cut eggs in half lengthwise and remove yolks. Mash. Melt butter, add onion and cook until softened. Add mushrooms then white wine, salt and pepper and cook until all the liquid has gone and mushrooms are soft. Remove from the heat; add mayonnaise, cream and mix this with the mashed egg yolks. Fill into the whites and press together; the filling should be rather heaped.

Sauce
60 g (2 oz) butter
2 tablespoons plain flour
2 cups milk
¼ teaspoon dry English-style mustard
salt and pepper
60 g (2 oz) finely chopped gruyère cheese

Melt butter; add flour; cook 1 minute until foaming. Add milk, seasonings and stir until boiling and thickened. Cook gently a couple of minutes. Remove from heat; add cheese and stir until melted. Check for seasoning. Pour a little sauce into a greased small shallow ovenproof dish. Place eggs on top, cover with more sauce. Bake in a moderate oven, 180-190°C (350-375°F), for 20 minutes until bubbling.
This dish is a very good entrée for 6 although quite rich and filling. For a luncheon it is best served with a salad platter.

Smoked Cod Balls with Mayonnaise and Mustard Sauce

250 g (½ lb) smoked cod
2 large potatoes (about 250 g or ½ lb)
60 g (2 oz) butter
1 large white onion, finely chopped
½ teaspoon curry powder
black pepper
salt if needed
1 large egg
a little plain flour

Place the cod in a saucepan; cover with cold water and bring to the boil. Cook very gently until just tender. Drain and flake into fine shreds, being careful to check for any bones. Cook the potatoes in salted water until tender and drain well. Put through *moulin* or mash. Mix with the cod. Melt butter and cook onion until softened; add curry and fry a minute. Mix into cod with salt and pepper if needed. Sometimes the cod can be quite salty, other times because of the addition of potato this dish needs a little extra seasoning. Beat in egg and leave to cool. Form into small balls and roll in flour. Fry a few at a time in hot oil until they rise to the surface and are golden brown in colour. Drain on paper towels and keep hot in the oven. Serve with mayonnaise and mustard sauce. Makes about 24-30 but this depends on how small they are.

Mayonnaise and Mustard Sauce
½ cup mayonnaise
1 tablespoon lemon juice
2 teaspoons hot English-style mustard
1 teaspoon French mustard
2 tablespoons lightly whipped cream

Mix all the ingredients. Keep sauce chilled. This can be made 12 hours beforehand.

Scotch Pastie with Butter and Lemon Sauce

750 g (1½ lb) smoked cod or blue cod
60 g (2 oz) butter
2 medium-sized white onions, diced
1 large green pepper, diced
1 large clove garlic, crushed
2 medium-sized ripe tomatoes.
1 egg
2 egg yolks
black pepper
salt (depending on the saltiness of the fish)
½ cup finely chopped parsley
¾ cup breadcrumbs, made from stale bread
500 g (1 lb) puff pastry
1 egg, beaten, to glaze

Cook the cod in water until tender. Drain. Remove carefully any bones. Flake and put in a large basin.
Melt the butter and cook onion, pepper and garlic until softened. Peel the tomatoes, chop finely and add. Cook this with the onion mixture just for a couple of minutes. Leave to cool a little. Add to the flaked fish. Mix in the egg, yolks, pepper, parsley and crumbs. It should not be too wet; if so, add a few more breadcrumbs. Roll puff pastry out thinly. Cut out 2 circles about the size of dinner plates. Divide the filling, placing it on one side of the circles only and fold the other side over just like you were making a pastie. Pinch the edges together and then glaze the top and edges with the beaten egg. Prick the top and keep chilled. It can be kept 12 hours at this stage in the refrigerator. Bake on a greased scone tray

in a moderate oven, 180-190°C (350-375°F), for about 25-30 minutes or until the pastry is golden brown and the filling is set.
Serve cut in slices with hot Butter and Lemon Sauce.

Butter and Lemon Sauce
Melt in a saucepan 90 g (3 oz) butter
Add ⅓ cup lemon juice
1 clove crushed garlic
1 teaspoon finely chopped capers
little black pepper

NUTS

While nuts are sold pre-packaged throughout the year and can be used at all times, the first of the nuts which are collected in autumn have the sweetest flavour of all. Surprisingly few people bother to grow walnut or almond trees; perhaps the work of shelling the nuts is too arduous a task. Other countries make a more creative use of the variety of nuts on the market, using them fried, or chopped, ground, or pounded in meat dishes, with rice, vegetables, fish and salads. Here they are mostly used in various biscuit and cake recipes.

For cakes the method of grinding nuts is important. The blender is quick and easy but can make nuts a little too oily; a hand-operated Mouli grater is best of all. This inexpensive little machine cuts the nuts into dry and tiny pieces which are powdery and light.

Walnut Crêpes with Chocolate Sauce

First make up about 18 crêpes. (It doesn't have to be exactly this number). Use basic crêpe recipe.

Filling
125 g (¼ lb) walnuts, finely ground
30 g (1 oz) butter
½ cup sugar
grated rind of 1 orange
1 tablespoon orange juice
1 tablespoon brandy

Place walnuts in a bowl. Melt butter and add, together with sugar, orange rind, juice and brandy.
Grease a round shallow ovenproof dish. Place down one crêpe, dot a little of the filling over this, then cover with another crêpe, more filling and so on until all are used. Melt a little extra bit of butter and brush the top.
Can be prepared 12 hours beforehand as long as it is well covered.
To Cook: Cover the top with foil and bake in moderate oven, 180-190°C (350-375°F), for about 20 minutes. Serve cut in wedges with Chocolate Sauce and ice cream. It is an extremely rich dessert so is mostly suitable for serving after a plain main course.

Chocolate Sauce
85 g (about 3 oz) dark chocolate
½ cup cream
1 teaspoon vanilla essence

Break the chocolate into pieces and place in a saucepan with cream and vanilla essence. Warm, stirring until the chocolate is melted and the sauce is quite smooth. It can be prepared beforehand and then just gently heated through at dinner time. If it goes too thick, add a spoonful of milk to thin it down.

Cheese Walnut Spread

125 g (¼ lb) grated cheese (1 cup) lightly packed
60 g (2 oz) Philadelphia cream cheese
2 teaspoons dry mustard
1 teaspoon Worcestershire sauce
salt and pepper
2 teaspoons dry sherry
2 tablespoons mayonnaise
2 tablespoons finely chopped walnuts

Mix all ingredients except the walnuts and mash well. Lastly mix in the nuts.

Nut Crescents

This quantity makes about 40

1 cup plain flour
2 tablespoons sugar
125 g (4 oz) butter
60 g (2 oz) almonds (unblanched)
1 egg yolk
little castor sugar to finish

Sift the plain flour into a basin. Add sugar. Cut butter into small pieces and rub in. Mince or grind the almonds and add with the egg yolk. Knead lightly until a soft consistency. It should be slightly moist and sticky. Take teaspoons of the mixture and roll out into crescents. Place these on a buttered scone tray. They can be put fairly close together as they don't spread. Bake in a moderate oven, 180-190°C (350-375°F), for about 12-15 minutes or until a pale golden colour. Remove carefully while warm using a spatula. Have a piece of paper ready with some castor sugar on it. Place each crescent on this and toss gently in the sugar. Put aside to cool and store when cold. They keep well for weeks in an airtight tin.

Walnut Roll

5 large eggs, separated
¾ cup sugar
¾ cup finely ground walnuts (about 90 g or 3 oz)
few drops vanilla

To Finish
1 cup cream
1 tablespoon castor sugar
1 tablespoon brandy
85 g (about 3 oz) dark chocolate

Separate eggs. Beat yolks with sugar until thick and lemon. Add nuts and a few drops of vanilla. Beat whites until very stiff. Fold through a quarter at a time. Grease a Swiss roll tin with butter. Line with a piece of paper and grease this also with butter. Sprinkle with flour and shake away the excess. Fill mixture into tin and bake in a moderate oven, 180-190°C (350-375°F), about 25 minutes or until golden, puffed and firm on top. Leave to cool a couple of minutes; turn out, remove paper and roll up in a piece of fresh waxed paper. Hold for a moment, gently, then unroll. When cool, cream.
Beat cream until stiff, add sugar and brandy and stir well. Fill into walnut roll. Trim ends neatly. Break the chocolate into pieces and melt standing in a basin over hot water. When smooth and running, spread over top and sides of roll and leave to set. If you wish, a layer of rosettes of cream can be piped down the top in a line. Use a sharp knife to cut through the chocolate, although it should only be a thin layer over the cake. This chocolate coating means the roll can be kept for a

day or so and the cake doesn't dry. The combination of brandy cream, delicate cake and crisp chocolate is quite superb. It can be used as a dessert cake or served with coffee.

Almond Torte with Coffee Cream

Serves 8

4 large egg whites
pinch cream of tartar
¾ cup castor sugar
90 g (3 oz) ground almonds (¾ cup)

Cover 2 scone trays with foil. Brush this with a little vegetable oil. Mark out 2 circles on the trays using a dinner plate about 23 cm or 9 inch. This can be done quite simply using a pencil. Beat the egg whites until stiff, adding cream of tartar. Add ½ cup of the castor sugar and beat until a stiff meringue. Mix the remaining sugar and ground almonds together and fold this through. Divide into 2 and spread out to cover the circles marked on the foil. Bake in a slow oven, 140-150°C (275-300°F), until crisp. Don't let it go too brown. It will crisp up even more as it cools. Remove from the foil carefully.

It is easiest to do this while the meringue is warm. Leave to cool and store in an airtight container, if not using immediately. It will keep several days.

Filling
1 tablespoon instant coffee
2 tablespoons boiling water
2 teaspoons gelatine
1 tablespoon cold water
2 large eggs
½ cup castor sugar
1 cup cream

Place the coffee in a cup and add boiling water. Stir until well mixed.

Mix gelatine and cold water together and stir. Stand over hot water and stir until dissolved. Mix with coffee. Separate the eggs, and beat yolks and sugar until very thick. Add coffee and mix.

Beat the whites until stiff and also the cream. Mix them together and fold the coffee mixture into this. Leave to firm up slightly in the refrigerator. Place 1 layer of almond meringue on a platter. Spread with coffee filling and top with remaining meringue layer. Press down gently and keep cold. It can be served as soon as the filling sets firmly or kept for 24 hours in the refrigerator. The meringue becomes soft but this doesn't detract from the sweet at all. If you would like the meringue crisp serve within several hours of making.

To Decorate
½ cup cream
2 tablespoons grated dark chocolate

Whip the cream and pipe a layer of rosettes around the edge of the torte. Dust these with the grated chocolate.

Hazelnut Snow Balls

Although these have equal quantities of almonds and hazelnuts, they are still called Hazelnut Snow Balls because this is the dominating flavour.
Firstly, lightly brush some small paper cases with a little vegetable oil.

60 g (2 oz) ground almonds (½ cup)
60 g (2 oz) ground hazelnuts (½ cup)
2 tablespoons icing sugar
2 egg whites
extra icing

Mix ground almonds and hazelnuts with sugar and add enough of the egg white to make a stiff, but moist, paste. Beat remaining egg white using a fork until frothy. Make mixture into tiny balls; dip first in egg white and then roll in extra icing sugar. Place in paper cases and bake in a moderate oven, 180-190°C (350-375°F), for 12-15 minutes. The centre should be soft and the outside crisp and golden. This makes about 15-18 and if you're strong-willed, they keep up to 4 weeks in an airtight jar.

Hazelnut Torte

Serves 8

This cake improves if made 24 hours before eating.

6 egg whites
pinch salt
10 tablespoons castor sugar
185 g (6 oz) hazelnuts, finely ground or minced
1 teaspoon white vinegar
½ teaspoon vanilla

Grease 2 sponge cake tins (20 cm or 8 inch in size). Cut out 2 pieces of plain white paper. Butter both tins; place in paper and butter this. Lightly flour the tin and paper, shaking away the excess.
Whip the egg whites and salt until stiff. Add 5 tablespoons of castor sugar and beat until mixture is like meringue. Fold in remaining 5 tablespoons. Add nuts, vinegar and vanilla and fold through. Divide this equally between the tins.
Bake in moderate oven, 180-190°C (350-375°F), until slightly crusty on top and just set. Cool for a few minutes and then turn out of the tin. Remove paper. These cakes can be kept in an airtight tin several days before filling.

Filling and Topping
1 cup cream
60 g (2 oz) dark chocolate

Whip the cream until stiff. Take out about 4 tablespoons and put this in a small basin. Break the chocolate into pieces and place in a basin or put on a plate and over a pan of hot water. When melted and smooth, add this to the 4 tablespoons of cream. Mix well. Spread this chocolate filling on 1 layer of the cake and then top with the other half. Spread the remainder of the cream over the top and sides.
If you wish a little extra grated chocolate can be sprinkled on top or else some extra melted chocolate piped over in a lattice. To do this you need another 60 g (2 oz).
Keep cake refrigerated, it is deliciously light but very rich.

Almond Tart

Serves 8

Pastry
1 cup flour
pinch salt
60 g (2 oz) butter
2 tablespoons castor sugar
2 egg yolks

Sift flour and salt together; put butter, sugar and yolks in centre and cream together, gradually mixing in dry ingredients. Knead until a soft mixture. Chill. This will keep 4 days. Roll out. Line flan tin (20 cm or 8 inch) and cut away edges.

Filling
⅓ cup apricot jam
3 egg yolks
½ teaspoon vanilla
¼ teaspoon almond essence
½ cup sugar
1 teaspoon orange rind
¾ cup cream
60 g (2 oz) ground almonds

Spread layer of jam in case. Beat yolks, vanilla, almond, sugar and rind. Add cream and almonds. Pour into case and bake 25-30 minutes in a moderate oven, 180-190°C (350-375°F). This goes quite a golden brown and will still be a little soft on top when you take it from the oven but as it cools, the filling becomes firm. Finish with a thin layer of cream before serving.

APPLES, PEARS AND A FIG DISH

Apples

A common phrase to denote something favourite or else the pick of the crop is 'the apple of one's eye', and this is applicable from a culinary point of view as they are a favourite in the kitchen, being invaluable for use in pies, dumplings, puddings, stuffings or eaten fresh.

They mainly fall into two groups — cooking apples which have a flesh which becomes soft and pulpy when cooked and is usually more acidic and eating apples, usually of smaller size, with a darker skin, while the Granny Smith is a wonderful variety which fits into either category as it is equally good for cooking and for eating.

When cooking try and avoid using huge quantities of water. If they are to be eaten warm or hot they have twice as much flavour if cooked in a little sugar and butter.

Muscat Spiced Apples

12 small eating apples
3 cups liqueur muscat
1 cup sugar
small piece cinnamon stick
rind 1 large orange grated
juice 1 orange
¼ cup brandy

Peel apples; cut in quarters and remove core. Place the muscat, sugar, cinnamon and orange rind in a pan. Warm this until the sugar is dissolved and then add the apples. Simmer, covered for about 1½ hours over very low heat until they are tender and a golden brown colour. Cool and then add the orange juice and brandy. Pour over the apples again and chill. This keeps well for 1 week. More brandy can be added if you wish before serving.
Serve plain or with cream.

Glazed Apples Flambé

6 cooking apples
½ cup water
1 cup white wine
1 tablespoon sugar
red currant jelly (about ½ cup)
a little light brown sugar
3 tablespoons brandy

Peel and cut the apples in four. Core. Bring water, wine and sugar to the boil in a saucepan. Add the apple sections. Cook, until just barely tender. Remove carefully with a spoon and place in a buttered shallow ovenproof dish. Melt down the red currant jelly in a saucepan and brush over the top of each apple quarter well with jelly. Sprinkle over this a tiny bit of light brown sugar. Exact quantities are hard but about ½ teaspoon should be enough for each apple section. Leave aside. This can be done several hours beforehand. Reheat in moderate oven, 180-190°C (350-375°F), for about 12 minutes or until glazed and hot. Warm the brandy in a small pot and pour over the apples. Light and serve immediately plain or with ice cream.

Apple Regency

4 sliced cooking apples
30 g (1 oz) butter
1 tablespoon sugar
2 tablespoons water
rind of 1 lemon
1 tablespoon brandy
3 tablespoons breadcrumbs (made from stale bread)

Place in saucepan, apples, butter, sugar and water. Cover and cook until apples are just barely softened. Don't overcook them. Add lemon rind and brandy. Leave to cool slightly. Add breadcrumbs.

30 g (1 oz) butter
3 tablespoons castor sugar
2 eggs (separated)
2 tablespoons castor sugar

Cream in a basin the butter and 3 tablespoons castor sugar; add egg yolks one at a time, then mix this with the apple. Beat egg whites until stiff; add 2 tablespoons castor sugar and beat until a stiff meringue. Fold this into the apple. Place in buttered ovenproof dish. Bake in moderate oven, 180-190°C (350-375°F), for 25-30 minutes.

Serve hot or warm with cream or ice cream.

Apple Pie

5 good sized cooking apples, peeled and cored
¾ cup sugar
2 tablespoons water
½ teaspoon cinnamon
1 tablespoon marmalade
30 g (1 oz) butter

Place the apples, sugar, water and cinnamon in a pan. Place the lid on and cook over medium heat and stir occasionally until they are softened. If very wet drain them lightly. Finally add the butter and marmalade and leave aside to cool. This can be kept in the refrigerator several days.

Pastry
155 g (5 oz) butter
2 tablespoons boiling water
1½ cups S.R. flour
pinch salt
1 packet blanched almonds (60 g or 2 oz)

Cut butter into small pieces and place in bowl. Cover with the water and mash the butter until softened. Don't worry if there is still a bit of water in the bowl. Add the flour sifted with salt. Mix to a paste with your fingers and then form into a ball. Knead it lightly until a soft mixture. Chill about ½ hour. Divide in half and roll out one half very thinly. If difficult to handle, roll between wax paper. Line base of a greased pie dish with half the crust. Fill the apple into this. Roll out the remaining pastry and place on top of apple. Pinch the edges. Brush the top lightly with a little milk and sprinkle with sugar. Arrange a layer of almonds around the edge and bake in a moderate oven, 180-190°C (350-375°F), for 30 minutes.

Serve hot or cool.

The pie can be made beforehand and reheated.

Apple and Hazelnut Kuchen

Serves 8

Crust
1 cup plain flour
¼ cup castor sugar
30 g (1 oz) hazelnuts, finely ground
60 g (2 oz) butter
1 large egg
grated rind of 1 lemon
½ teaspoon vanilla essence

Sift flour into a bowl, add sugar and hazelnuts and mix together. Cut butter into tiny pieces and using the fingertips, mix until it resembles meal. Add egg, lemon rind and vanuilla essence to the centre; mix and knead until it forms a workable mixture. Roll out to a large circle and press into lightly buttered spring form tin about 23 cm (9 inch) in size. The majority of spring form tins are very deep. If this is the case with yours, the mixture will reach about half way up the side of the tin. If you don't have a spring form tin, use a flan ring. Leave to chill while preparing the filling.

Apple Filling
500 g (1 lb) cooking apples
1 tablespoon lemon juice
¼ cup sugar
½ teaspoon cinnamon

Peel and core the apples and cut in very thin slices. Place in a large basin and mix in lemon juice, sugar and cinnamon. Toss the mixture. Place in hazelnut case and press down gently.

Topping
30 g (1 oz) hazelnuts, finely ground
2 tablespoons white sugar
1 tablespoon brown sugar
30 g (1 oz) butter, melted

Mix nuts and sugar together. Stir through melted butter. Spread over the top of the apples. Bake in moderate oven, 180-190°C (350-375°F), for 35 minutes until the case is golden and the apples are tender.
Cool and reheat as needed.

To Serve
1 tablespoon brandy

Warm the brandy and light. Pour this over the top of the tart.

Apricot Nut Kuchen

Use 500 g (1 lb) apricots; stone them and cut in quarters. They need to be fairly ripe ones without being mushy. In this case use almonds, finely ground for the pastry case and the topping.

Peach Nut Kuchen

Use 500 g (1 lb) ripe, yellow peaches. Stone them and cut in thin slices and proceed as before. You can either use hazelnuts or almonds: the hazelnuts have a fairly dominant flavour with the peaches but it is still a good combination. Otherwise use almonds and orange or lemon rind.
These tarts are nicest served with a bowl of sweetened whipped cream.

Pears Alicia (see p. 98)

Apple Mousse with Orange Sauce

Unlike the majority of recipes in the book which serve 6, this recipe makes 8-10 generous servings.

However it is easy to halve the recipe or double it for a party dessert.

It keeps well, provided it is well covered, for about 36 hours in the refrigerator and the mousse has a lovely fresh, tart apple flavour, interesting when combined with the orange.

1 kg (2 lb) cooking apples
grated rind of 1 lemon
4 tablespoons brown sugar
3 tablespoons apricot jam
30 g (1 oz) butter
1 tablespoon gelatine
2 tablespoons lemon juice
2 eggs
2 egg yolks
½ cup (4 oz) caster (powdered) sugar
1 tablespoon Grand Marnier
2 tablespoons brandy
1¼ cups (10 fl oz) cream

Peel the apples, core them and cut into thin slices. Place them into a saucepan with the lemon rind, brown sugar, apricot jam and butter. Cover tightly and place over medium heat. You must stir these occasionally or they may stick, especially in the first ten minutes of cooking until the juices start to flow from the apples. Once they are moist, leave them to cook for 25 to 30 minutes or until they are quite soft.

Mix the gelatine with some water and place this over hot water to dissolve.

When the apple is ready puree it, either in a moulin, sieve or a food processor. Mix the dissolved gelatine into the apple, add the lemon juice and leave aside to cool for about 20 minutes. Don't let the apple set.

Beat the eggs and egg yolks with the caster sugar until thick and pale in colour. This is easiest in an electric mixer. Stir the eggs into the apple mousse.

Add the Grand Marnier and brandy. Whip ½ cup of the cream until it holds soft peaks then fold it into the apple mixture.

Pour into either individual dishes or else into a larger dish and chill until set.

Orange Sauce

2 tablespoons apricot jam
½ cup (4 fl oz) orange juice
1 tablespoon Grand Marnier
4 oranges

For the best flavour, make the sauce several hours before you serve it. It can be kept covered in the refrigerator for 12 hours.

Place the apricot jam and orange juice into a small saucepan and warm it over low heat. When the jam has melted pour the mixture through a sieve to remove any pieces of apricot and add the Grand Marnier. Leave to cool.

Peel the oranges, being careful to remove all the white pith.

Using a small sharp knife cut out the segments.

Add these to the sauce. It may look like a small quantity, but the orange segments will produce more juice as the sauce stands.

Whip the remaining cream until it holds stiff peaks, don't sweeten it as the sauce has sufficient sweetening. If the oranges had a tart flavour the use of the apricot jam counteracts this.

Place the cream into a piping bag with a star tube and pipe a lattice of cream over the top of the individual desserts or the large dish.

Serve the orange sauce at the table.

Pears

The pear has been cultivated for so many centuries — since long before the Christian era — that at least six thousand varieties have been named. However, not all of these six thousand are now in existence.

In China, or so the story goes, they once grew a pear which weighed a good ten pounds, and despite the large size had a very white flesh and good fragrance. In Jersey, one of the Channel Islands, pears have often been grown up to five pounds in weight, and these sell on the market at about six dollars each.

Most pears are picked before they are ripe, for tree ripened fruit has a tendency to become coarse in taste and gritty. This fruit is delicious if eaten just at the moment of ripeness, but once past this peak becomes mushy rather than juicy and smooth. If you want to use them in cooking choose fruit that is firm and still slightly under-ripe.

Pears Alicia

6 to 8 eating pears (buy pears that are slightly under-ripe)
1 cup water
1 cup sugar
1 cup sweet sherry
peel of orange, cut in strips
¼ cup brandy
¼ cup curacao

Peel pears, leaving stalks on. Place water, sugar, sweet sherry and orange peel in a large pot. When sugar is dissolved, add the pears; cover and cook over gentle heat until they are tender. This should be done slowly and usually takes about 1½ hours. The longer it takes the nicer they are. They can be turned every so often, especially if any are out of the liquid. Eventually they turn a glorious golden colour and become very glazed and transparent. When tender, leave to cool. Keep chilled. Add the curacao and brandy just before serving. If added days beforehand, this tends to evaporate away. They keep well for a week.

French Pears

6 eating pears
30 g (1 oz) butter
2 tablespoons sugar
½ cup cream
2 tablespoons brandy

Peel, quarter and core the pears. Place in a saucepan with the butter and sugar. Cover and cook over gentle heat, shaking the pan occasionally until the pears are tender. This depends on how firm they were. Lastly add the cream and brandy and keep warm until serving. This dish can also be made in the morning and reheated gently.

Glazed Figs

18 small ripe figs (allow about 3 per person)
1½ cups red wine
¾ cup sugar
¼ cup water
juice of 1 lemon
¼ cup brandy

Carefully peel the figs. Heat the wine, sugar and water in a saucepan. Add the figs and cover. Cook over very low heat for only a couple of minutes. If ripe, be careful they don't break up. Leave aside for a few minutes with the lid on the pot and then using a spoon, carefully remove them to a bowl. Boil the liquid until it is slightly reduced. Add the lemon and brandy and pour over the figs. Leave to cool.
Serve very cold with cream and small biscuits.
These improve by being left for about 24 hours in the liquid before serving.

Winter

WINTER SOUPS

Je vis de bonne soupe et non de beau language.
'I live by good soup and not by fine words' — so stated Chrysale in Molier's *Les Femmes Savantes.*
On cold winter days, a soup bowl filled with steaming savoury soup renders words quite unnecessary.

Onion and Tomato Soup Beaureconne

Mention the word onion soup and even the most unsophisticated people think of France. It is possibly one of the most celebrated and well known of all the world's soups. But of course it is only one of a whole repertoire of onion soups which come from areas all over Europe. This is a variation of onion soup (named after the fertile area of Beauce — west of Paris) containing as well as the onions, tomatoes, parsley and spices, making a rich and fragrant soup.

60 g (2 oz) butter
3 large white onions, thinly sliced
1 clove garlic crushed
a couple of sprigs of parsley, chopped
½ bay leaf
pinch dried thyme
pinch cloves
1 tablespoon brandy
4 cups beef stock (or else use 1 tin beef consomme, size 425 g or 14-15 oz and 1 tin water)
2 large ripe tomatoes, peeled

Melt butter and add onion. Sauté until golden. Add garlic, parsley, bay leaf, thyme and cloves. Add brandy, warm for a moment and light. Add beef stock and cover; cook gently for 30 minutes.
Chop the tomatoes into tiny pieces and add.
Cook another 10 minutes, remove bay leaf and check for seasoning.
This soup keeps well for several days.

Chicken Soup with Mixed Vegetables and Savoury Chicken Balls

30 g (1 oz) butter
1 tablespoon oil
2 strips bacon, diced
1 diced white onion
1 small carrot, diced
1 stalk celery, diced
1 green pepper, cut in strips
2 mushrooms diced
4 cups chicken stock
1 diced potato
½ tin sweet corn kernels
2 ripe tomatoes, peeled and cut in small pieces
½ cup cream
1 tablespoon dry sherry
1 tablespoon chopped parsley

Heat butter and oil; cook bacon, onion, carrot, celery, pepper, mushrooms, till soft. Add stock, potato, sweet corn and tomato. Cook until potato is tender. Lastly, add cream, sherry and parsley.
Serve with savoury chicken balls on top.
This chicken soup is best kept only a short time (about 24 hours).

Savoury Chicken Balls
30 g (1 oz) butter
1 white onion, finely diced
¼ teaspoon curry powder
1 cup cooked chicken
salt and pepper
2 teaspoons cornflour
1 small egg white
extra cornflour

Melt butter and sauté onion until softened. Add curry and cook a couple of minutes gently. Place chopped chicken in a small bowl; add onion mixture, cornflour and egg white. The mixture must be very well seasoned. Form into small balls and roll in extra cornflour. Flatten slightly.

To Cook
1 tablespoon vegetable oil
15 g (½ oz) butter

Heat oil and butter and when foaming add chicken balls, cook turning once until golden on the outside. These can be cooked beforehand and then reheated in the oven for a minute. Float a couple on top of each bowl of soup.

Mushroom Soup

60 g (2 oz) butter
1 large white onion finely chopped
250 g (½ lb) mushrooms
1 tablespoon flour
3 cups chicken stock
1 cup cream
salt and pepper to taste

Melt the butter and sauté onion until softened but not brown. Keep aside two small mushrooms for the garnish. Chop the remainder into dice. Add to the onion and cook gently about 10 minutes. Add flour and stir; add stock and cook 20 minutes. Put the soup in a blender or through a fine *moulin.* Add cream and check for seasoning.
To Serve: Cut the 2 mushrooms which you kept aside into thin slices. Add them to the soup and warm through for about 1 minute. Don't overcook them as they should still have a firm texture.

Cream of Carrot and Tomato Soup

60 g (2 oz) butter
1 large white onion, finely chopped
500 g (1 lb) sliced carrots
1 tin tomatoes (about 450 g or 14-15 oz)
4 cups chicken stock
salt, pepper and pinch sugar
½ cup cream

Melt butter, sauté onion until golden, add carrots and cook until golden. This preliminary cooking adds to the flavour of the soup. Add tomatoes and chicken, stock, salt, pepper and sugar. Cover and cook gently about 45 minutes. Then put through a *moulin,* sieve or blender. Reheat; add the cream before serving and stir. Sprinkle the top of each serve with 1 teaspoon finely chopped parsley or chives.
Keeps 2 days refrigerated.

Hungarian Style Beef Soup

500 g (1 lb) stewing beef, cut in very tiny cubes
30 g (1 oz) butter
1 large diced onion
1 clove garlic
1 tablespoon sweet paprika
1 tin beef consomme (425 g or 14-15 oz) ⎫ mixed together
1 tin water
½ teaspoon salt
pepper
2 large, ripe tomatoes, peeled and cut in small pieces
1 large green pepper, cut in tiny strips
1 medium-sized potato, cut in small cubes

Cut all the fat away from the meat and be sure it really is cut up small. This takes time but is worth the effort as the soup is spoilt if there are great big lumps of meat in it. Melt butter and fry onion and garlic until softened. Remove pan from the heat; add paprika and stir. Return to the heat; add meat and cook until it has changed colour. Add consomme, pepper and salt and cook until the meat is tender — about 45 minutes. Add tomatoes, green pepper and potato and cook another ½ hour or until vegetables are tender. Leave to cool and then remove fat before serving.

Potage Paul

30 g (1 oz) butter
1 white onion, finely diced
1 clove garlic, chopped
3 large lettuce leaves, chopped
2 tablespoons parsley, chopped
½ teaspoon curry powder
4 cups chicken stock
2 tablespoons dried surprise peas
2 teaspoons cornflour mixed with
1 tablespoon water
½ cup cream

Melt the butter, cook onion, garlic, lettuce, parsley until softened. Add curry and fry a moment. Add stock, peas and cook covered for 30 minutes. *Moulin* or vitamise soup. Add the cornflour and water and stir until lightly thickened. Lastly add cream and taste for seasoning.
This keeps for 2 days refrigerated.

Lentil Soup

8-10 Serves

1 cup lentils
4 cups chicken stock
1 bay leaf
60 g (2 oz) butter
1 large white onion, finely diced
1 tin tomatoes, chopped (size about 425 g)
1 medium-sized potato, diced
2 continental frankfurts
1 tablespoon finely chopped parsley

I prefer to use the pink coloured lentils, not so much for flavour, but they make a more attractive soup in colour.
Place lentils and chicken stock in a large saucepan with the bay leaf. Simmer covered for about 1¼ hours. Stir the lentils until they are almost puréed or else

put through a sieve. Melt the butter, cook the onion until softened. Add to the soup with the chopped tomatoes and potato and simmer another 45 minutes. This keeps well for several days refrigerated.

To Serve: Heat the soup again. Slice the frankfurts thinly and add; cook 1 minute and serve with parsley on top.

Seafood Chowder

30 g (1 oz) butter
1 rasher bacon, chopped finely
1 stalk celery, chopped finely
1 green pepper, cut in thin strips
1 small white onion, diced finely
1 cup prawn stock
1 small potato, peeled and cut in cubes
1 cup milk
250 g (½ lb) prawns, shelled and cut in halves
250 g (½ lb) scallops, cleaned and cut in slices
¼ cup cream

To Garnish
a little finely chopped parsley
sprinkle of sweet paprika

Melt butter; add bacon, celery, pepper and onion and sauté until vegetables are softened. Add prawn stock and potato; cover and cook gently until the vegetables are tender. Add milk, prawns and scallops. Remove from the heat and leave to stand for a few minutes to bring out the flavours. Reheat for serving, being careful not to overcook and toughen the seafood. When hot add cream; then garnish with parsley and paprika (seasoning for soup depends on the saltiness of the prawns, so taste first).

Prawn Stock: Shell the prawns. Place heads and shells in a saucepan. Cover with 1½ cups water, little salt and cook gently, covered for about 1 hour. Strain and press down to extract all the flavour from the shells.

AVOCADO

This is distinctive for its nutty flavour and buttery texture and unusual in the fact that it can adapt itself to every course from hors d'oeuvre through to dessert. The amount of oil in the avocado increases as the fruit matures and in general, the greater the percentage of oil, the better the flavour. They mature on the tree but soften only after being picked. Unfortunately, they bruise easily and are often ruined when you buy them by the pokes and pinches of inquisitive shoppers. The best test for ripeness is to press the fruit gently between the palms of the hand. When it gives slightly, it is ready to eat.

Avocado can be obtained throughout the year but varies in quality and price. It is usually more easily obtained at peak quality in the winter months, or late autumn.

Ripe avocado pulp darkens when exposed for a while to air unless given a protective coating of lemon juice. It can be heated through, but prolonged cooking ruins its flavour.

103

Avocado Omelette

This quantity makes 2 large omelettes or 4 small ones

60 g (2 oz) butter
1 small white onion, finely diced
½ teaspoon curry powder
2 teaspoons finely chopped parsley
1 small ripe avocado
4 large eggs
½ teaspoon salt
2 tablespoons water
1 tablespoon tomato sauce

Melt the butter and cook onion until softened. Add curry and fry 1 minute; add parsley. Peel the avocado and dice flesh into small pieces. Add to onion and cook for only 1 minute. Leave to cool. Place the eggs, salt, water and tomato sauce in a basin and beat well with a fork. Add the cooled avocado mixture and stir. This can be covered and kept refrigerated for as long as 8 hours without spoiling.

To Make Up Omelettes: Heat a pan, when very hot add 1 walnut-sized piece of butter; it should sizzle immediately. Pour in some of the egg and avocado mixture and shake gently until just set. It should only take a couple of minutes. While still moist on top, roll over and turn out on to a warmed plate. Each one must be eaten as soon as it is made, otherwise if kept warm in the oven they toughen and spoil.

Hawaii Dip

1 small ripe avocado
2 teaspoons lemon juice
1 tablespoon peanut or vegetable oil
¼ teaspoon salt, little black pepper
3 teaspoons horseradish relish
2 tablespoons mango and paw paw chutney

Mash the avocado with a silver fork. Gradually add the lemon juice and the oil. Season with salt, pepper and horseradish. If the mango and paw paw chutney has large pieces of fruit in it, mash or cut these finely. Add last, and then taste for seasoning. Either fill this dip back into the avocado shells or fill into a small bowl. Score the top with the prongs of a fork. Cover and keep refrigerated. It is best used within about 6 hours of making.

Serve either with fingers of hot toast or as a dip with potato crisps.

LEEKS AND ENDIVE

Leeks

Leeks would be one of the oldest of all vegetables. It is a rather taken-for-granted vegetable used more as an additional ingredient in a recipe than as a specialty on its own. The national emblem of Wales, they are accredited with giving extra depth and quality to the voice, and who am I to argue with that. After all, look at Richard Burton.

BASIC PREPARATION: Leeks are one of the dirtiest of all vegetables and must be carefully cleaned. Trim off the root and the coarse green part of the leaves, being careful to remove any withered ones. Slit the green part of the leek in several places and cut them to approximately the same length. Hold under running water for a few seconds and then leave heads downwards in a jug of cold water, so that any remaining grit will have seeped out. Lay in a saucepan and pour in just enough water to come about halfway up. Season with a little salt and place over a high heat. Cook until just softened. Check the white part of the leek with the point of a knife for tenderness. They usually take about 30 minutes to cook, but it depends, of course, on whether they are thin ones or thick ones. Drain well and press down gently to remove the excess water.

Leeks in Prawn Sauce

2 bunches leeks

Dressing
6 tablespoons oil
2 tablespoons white vinegar
½ teaspoon salt
black pepper
2 teaspoons French mustard
2 tablespoons finely chopped parsley
¼ teaspoon sugar
250 g (½ lb) prawns, peeled and deveined

Wash leeks and cook until just soft. Drain well. Mix together oil, white vinegar, salt, pepper, mustard, parsley and sugar. Chop the prawns into very tiny pieces and add. Pour this over the leeks while they are still warm. Leave to cool.
These are nicest if served at room temperature.
Serve as a first course with brown bread and butter triangles.

Leek Quiche

Sour Cream Pastry: This is a very light and fine pastry which can be made up and kept refrigerated for days. It is good for any savoury tart as it has a slightly flakey texture.

1 cup plain flour
pinch salt
125 g (4 oz) butter
2 tablespoons sour cream

Sift the flour with salt into a large basin, cut in the butter using 2 knives, and when a crumbly mixture, add sour cream. Mix well and knead lightly. Roll out wafer thin and press into a lightly greased flan tin sized about 25 cm (10 inch). Prick the base. Bake blind. Line with a piece of waxed paper; fill this with beans or rice and bake in moderate oven, 180-190°C (350-375°F), until set (about 25 minutes). Remove paper and beans. Return to the oven for a couple of minutes to dry the case, as it's a bit moist in the centre usually.

Filling
1 bunch leeks
60 g (2 oz) butter
½ cup finely diced ham
1 cup cream
¼ teaspoon salt
pepper
2 large eggs
2 tablespoons grated tasty cheese

Wash and clean the leeks. It is best to use mostly the white part in this dish. Cut it in thin slices. Melt butter and cook the sliced leek until softened. Mix with the ham. Beat together cream, eggs, salt and pepper and cheese. Add to leeks and pour mixture into tart case. Bake in moderate oven, 180-190°C (350-375°F), for 25 minutes or until set on top.
This is equally good piping hot, warm or cold.

Leeks in Bacon and Cream Sauce

2 bunches leeks
3 rashers bacon, rind removed and chopped small
60 g (2 oz) butter
½ teaspoon salt
black pepper
1 teaspoon paprika
1 cup sour cream
1 tablespoon lemon juice
finely chopped parsley

Wash leeks and cut into thin rings.
Fry the bacon in a pan and remove when crisp. Melt the butter in the same pan and add leeks. Sauté until softened, then add salt, pepper and paprika and stir for about 30 seconds over the heat. Add sour cream, lemon and warm through. Just before serving mix in bacon and heat until it has just heated through again. Serve immediately sprinkled with parsley.
Nice enough to be served as a dish on its own, or otherwise it goes best with plainly cooked meat dishes.

Belgian Endive

A Belgian gardener discovered by chance the leaves of Belgian endive. He worked for the Brussels Botanical Gardens and while searching for a coffee substitute found the delicate white leaves sprouting from a chicory root in his basement. He left the coffee project and began the cultivation of one of Belgium's most popular exports. This occured more than a century and a half ago and since that time this delicate vegetable has become known all over the world. It has only a short season, but is good both cooked and in salads, and is well worth trying as a change from the better known winter vegetables.

Unfortunately this vegetable has a confusing variety of names, being known as either Belgian Endive, Chicory or Witloof.

BASIC METHOD OF COOKING: Select plump and white heads, avoiding any that are beginning to go green as they will taste rather bitter. Cut away the hard piece at the bottom and then remove the pointed core with the tip of a sharp knife. This is the very bitter part of the Endive.
Place endive in a pan of salted water and bring to the boil, cook gently about 10 minutes. Drain well. As endive absorbs a lot of water it needs to be gently squeezed inside kitchen paper or in a clean towel. Transfer to a pan and cook gently in 30 g (1 oz) of butter until softened and slightly golden, seasoning with salt and pepper. It can be cooked beforehand in the water and then reheated in the butter later.
The vegetable has a slightly bitter taste, if you don't like this add 1 teaspoon sugar to the water when cooking it.

Endive and Onions

60 g (2 oz) butter
3 white onions, cut in half, and then in thin slices
salt and pepper
1 tablespoon white wine

Melt the butter and sauté onion until softened, seasoning with salt, pepper and white wine.

500 g (1 lb) endive
a small piece of butter
sprinkle of salt
½ teaspoon sugar
1 tablespoon water
2 teaspoons lemon juice

Wash the endive. Butter the base of a saucepan. Arrange the endive heads in a single layer on this. Mix together, salt, sugar, water and lemon juice and trickle this over the top. Weight them down with a plate; cover the pan and cook over a very low heat until they are tender (about 25 minutes should be enough). Remove the plate; add the onion mixture, cover again and leave 5 minutes for the onions to heat through and the endive to become quite tender. Remove carefully and arrange on a heated platter.

To Garnish
2 rashers bacon

Cut the bacon in tiny pieces. Place in a pan and cook until it is crispy. Sprinkle this over the endive and onion just before serving.

Belgian Endive with Cheese and Ham

1 cup water
2 teaspoons lemon juice
½ teaspoon salt
1 teaspoon sugar (optional)
6 endive
6 thin slices ham

NOTE: The sugar counteracts the slightly bitter taste of the endive and is optional.
Place the water, lemon, salt and sugar (if using) in a saucepan. Add the endive and cook rapidly for about 10 minutes. Drain well and carefully press out the liquid. Wrap each endive in a slice of ham and place in a shallow, buttered, ovenproof dish.
Make sauce.

Sauce
30 g (1 oz) butter
1 tablespoon plain flour
1 cup milk
salt and pepper
pinch nutmeg
60 g (2 oz) finely diced gruyère cheese
3 tablespoons breadcrumbs
30 g (1 oz) butter

Melt 30 g (1 oz) of the butter; add flour and cook a moment. Add the milk; stir until boiling; add salt, pepper and nutmeg. Remove from the heat and add the cheese. Stir until melted. Pour over the endive. Sprinkle the breadcrumbs over this and dot with the remaining butter. Bake in a moderate oven, 180-190°C (350-375°F), until golden. It takes about 20 minutes.
This dish can be prepared in the morning and reheated.

Endive and Orange Salad

3 medium-sized endive
3 oranges
½ bunch watercress

Cut the base from the endive. Separate and remove the leaves, stopping when you come to the centre core. Cut each piece of endive into long strips. Wash well and drain. Chill until crisp.
Peel the oranges and cut out the segments individually so no membrane or fibres are remaining. Keep aside, chilled. Wash the watercress and remove the stalks. Keep the heads chilled also. Just before serving, mix endive, orange and watercress in a large bowl, moistening with dressing.

Dressing
6 tablespoons oil
2 tablespoons white vinegar or lemon juice
little salt and pepper
pinch sugar

Mix all dressing ingredients together.
Endive, while delicious hot, is also one of the best of all winter salads; crisp and juicy, it can be combined with other ingredients, served on its own or with lettuce.

SOME OTHER WINTER VEGETABLES

Cauliflower

This is actually an Oriental vegetable and reached Europe via Cyprus. It still plays a part in Chinese cooking and is used particularly in India. It is eaten in many guises in France where it is called *Chous fleurs*, in Spain with grated orange rind, in Dijon with a mustard sauce, in Vienna with ham and sour cream, in Amsterdam with hollandaise sauce, in Scandinavia with dill sauce and in Australia, mostly with either white or cheese sauce.

BASIC METHOD OF COOKING: Choose firm and white heads when buying. Cut the flowerets off the stems. Cut the central thick stem into slices and wash. Drop into a large saucepan of salted boiling water and cook uncovered until it is tender but not mushy. Drain into a colander and if not serving or using immediately, place this into a large basin of cold water. This prevents further cooking so it keeps a fresh taste and texture.

Cauliflower Puff

1 small cauliflower or ½ large one

Cook in a pot of salted water until just tender. Drain well and either mash or else put through a *moulin.*
Mix into this cauliflower purée:

1 whole egg
¼ cup grated tasty cheese
2 tablespoons soft breadcrumbs
1 teaspoon Worcestershire sauce
1 teaspoon dry English-style mustard
¼ teaspoon salt, little pepper
½ cup cream

Mix all ingredients well and spoon into a greased ovenproof dish. I use a 4 cup soufflé dish for it, but any deep casserole would do. This can be prepared several hours beforehand and refrigerated. Cover well as it smells quite strong and could

flavour other foods in the refrigerator. Reheat in a moderate oven, 180-190°C (350-375°F), for about 25-30 minutes or until puffed and just firm on top.
Serve either plain or with cheese sauce.
This can be used as an accompanying vegetable or as a course on its own. Cooked this way the cauliflower becomes very delicate in flavour.

Cheese Sauce

30 g (1 oz) butter
1 tablespoon flour
1½ cups milk
¼ teaspoon dry English mustard
pepper, salt, pinch nutmeg
½ cup grated gruyère cheese

Melt the butter and add the flour. Cook a moment until foaming but not brown. Add the milk and stir continuously until thickened and boiling. Season with mustard, pepper, salt and nutmeg. Turn down the heat and simmer gently for about 5 minutes. Remove from the heat, add the cheese and stir until the cheese is melted. It should be very smooth and glossy.
Serve immediately.

Cauliflower in Mustard Sauce

1 small cauliflower or ½ large one

Sauce
60 6 (2 oz butter
2 tablespoons plain flour
2 cups milk
1 tablespoon dry English-style mustard
2 teaspoons French mustard
1 tablespoon mayonnaise
½ teaspoon salt
1 tablespoon lemon juice
4 tablespoons soft breadcrumbs
an extra 2 tablespoons melted butter

Cook the cauliflower in salted water until just tender. Drain and arrange in a shallow, ovenproof dish. Melt the butter, add the flour and cook until foaming but not brown. Add the milk, stir continuously until thickened and boiling. Mix in a small basin the mustards, mayonnaise, salt and lemon juice. Add this to the sauce and simmer gently for a few minutes. Use a spoon to evenly coat the cauliflower with the sauce. Sprinkle over the breadcrumbs and lastly trickle over the extra melted butter. Bake in moderate oven, 180-190°C (350-375°F), for about 12-15 minutes or until the top is golden. Or else it can be made in the morning and then reheated at dinner time for 20-25 minutes. This is really nice enough to be a small separate course on its own.

Cabbage

When George Bernard Shaw was a young drama critic it was the custom for the audience in the galleries to throw sausages at those critics whose tastes had offended them. On one such occasion he urged these irritable theatre goers not to throw sausages at him, not because he minded being knocked on the noggin by a sausage, but because he was a vegetarian. He suggested they hit him with something he could enjoy eating, for instance a cabbage.

Surprising, for mostly the cabbage is the butt of jokes, nasty stories and slurs about its aroma, appearance and taste. In the third century it was believed to be a cure for drunkenness and the Greek writer Athenaeus mentioned that the Egyptians who indulged in too much wine made it a habit to eat plenty of boiled cabbage before attending a feast. His words went something like this:

> Wife, quick, some cabbage boil, of virtues healing
> That I may rid me of this seedy feeling.

It may not be a cure for anything, especially a hangover, but it is a hardy vegetable, and when well cooked and flavoured in various ways, makes a delicious and interesting dish.

Savoury Cabbage

½ cabbage
60 g (2 oz) butter
1 diced rasher bacon
1 diced white onion
2 hard boiled eggs
little extra salt and pepper
2 tablespoons tasty cheese grated

Remove the coarse outside leaves and any damaged ones from the cabbage. Shred, removing the core and wash. Place in a saucepan with a little salt (I add a couple of teaspoons of sugar near the end of the cabbage season to help take away any strong taste). Cook about 10 minutes or until slightly crisp. Shake the saucepan occasionally to prevent it catching. Drain any excess liquid away.

Meantime melt the butter and cook the bacon and onion in this until the onion is softened. Mix with the cooked cabbage. Roughly chop the hard boiled eggs and add, seasoning with salt and pepper. Butter an ovenproof dish and add the cabbage; cover the top with the grated cheese and brown in a moderate oven, 180-190°C (350-375°F). It should take about 20 minutes to heat through.

Savoury Cabbage Roll

This is good served for lunch or as en entrée.

1 quantity Savoury Cabbage
1 large egg, or 2 small
250 g (½ lb) puff pastry
1 small egg to glaze
pinch salt

When preparing the savoury cabbage, instead of covering with grated cheese mix this through. When the cabbage is cold bind with the egg.

Roll puff pastry out very thinly to make a long oblong piece about the size of a Swiss roll tin. Spread down one side with the cabbage. Roll over to enclose and tuck in the ends. Brush all over with the small egg, beaten with a pinch of salt. Prick the top in several places and place the roll on a buttered scone tray. Refrigerate. It can be kept at this stage for 8 hours. Bake in a moderately hot oven, 190-200°C (375-400°F), for about 20-25 minutes or until golden brown and puffed. Serve cut in thick slices with a little melted butter or a jug of sour cream.

Steamed Cabbage Quarters

1 small wedge of cabbage for each person
salt
sugar
60 g (2 oz) butter
black pepper

This is a very simple but good way of cooking cabbage. It must be very fresh and young and not one bought near the end of the season.

Rinse the wedges. Drain lightly and sprinkle each one with a little salt and a pinch of sugar. Place in a colander and stand it over a large pan of boiling water. Cover with a lid. Steam over a moderate heat for about 25 minutes or until just tender. Lift the wedges out carefully and place on a warm plate. Melt the butter and pour over the top. Sprinkle with a little black pepper.

If more than 6 wedges are needed it is difficult to fit them in a colander and so this method becomes impractical.

Sweet Sour Red Cabbage

Red cabbage is one of the few vegetables which can be reheated successfully a day after preparing and it is delicious with veal, pork or poultry.

½ small red cabbage
60 g (2 oz) butter
1 large white onion, finely chopped
1 cooking apple, peeled and diced
1 teaspoon salt
¼ cup water
4 tablespoons red wine
1 tablespoon brown sugar

Remove the coarse outer leaves of the cabbage, cut out the core and shred finely. Wash.

Melt the butter, add onion and cook until golden. Add cabbage and cook, stirring occasionally about 10 minutes. Add apples, salt, water, cover and cook over low heat for about 1 hour.

When cabbage is tender add the red wine and brown sugar and simmer another 5 minutes.

Sprouts

Somebody once remarked 'The English have only two vegetables, cabbage and potato' and was corrected, 'No, they have three, two of them are cabbage and the other potato.' The other cabbage referred to was, of course, the Brussels sprout, that delicate but much abused vegetable which develops a strong stale odour and taste if overcooked. They are the most individual members of the cabbage family and should be picked when very small and tender with compactly packed leaves and small uniform size.

BASIC METHOD OF COOKING: Discard any wilted yellow outside leaves. Trim away the excess stem. Pierce a cross in it for more even cooking. Wash them rapidly in water and drain. Bring a pot of salted water to the boil, drop in the sprouts and bring up to the boil again as quickly as possible. Cook gently until just done. Check by piercing the stem of one with a knife. Drain well and plunge quickly into cold water. Drain again. Leave to become quite cold and then keep refrigerated. If not overcooked, they can be kept 24 hours and reheated in a little butter, salt and pepper.

Sprouts in Curry Cream

500 g (1 lb) small sprouts

Boil sprouts in salted water for a few minutes until just tender. Drain and chop in half.

60 g (2 oz) butter
1 white onion, diced
1 teaspoon curry
½ cup cream

Melt butter, cook the onion till soft, add curry, and fry a minute. Add sprouts and toss. Lastly add cream and cook until the cream has almost vanished and is just a thick mixture over the sprouts.

Broccoli

The broccoli plant which grows with the flower buds that form at the ends of the main and secondary stalks is not only a type of cauliflower but also a variety of cabbage. When buying, if the heads are beginning to show signs of yellow flowers, leave it; the broccoli is definitely too old to be any good.

BASIC PREPARATION: Divide the broccoli into flowerets and if the ends of the stalks are very coarse and thick, peel with a vegetable peeler. Cut the stalks into pieces. Cook the stems first for about 5 minutes in salted water, then add the flowerets. Drain when tender. Use a sharp knife to pierce one of the stems to check it.

Broccoli Soup

30 g (1 oz) butter
1 white onion, finely chopped
1 clove garlic, crushed
2 tablespoons finely chopped parsley
6 cups beef stock
1 tablespoon tomato paste
1 bunch broccoli
½ cup cooked macaroni
1 tablespoon grated parmesan cheese

Melt butter, cook onion, garlic, parsley until onion is softened. Add stock and tomato paste. Cut the broccoli flowerets in pieces and add. (When out of season this soup can be made using 1 packet of frozen broccoli (280 g or 9 oz). Simmer about 30 minutes. Sieve. Add cooked macaroni and heat.
Just before serving, stir in parmesan and check seasoning.

Purée of Broccoli

1 bunch fresh broccoli
60 g (2 oz) butter
1 teaspoon plain flour
little salt and pepper
1 tablespoon cream

Cook the broccoli until just tender and drain well. Press through a *moulin* or sieve. Keep aside until dinner time. If you refrigerate this be sure to cover it as it has quite a strong smell.
Melt butter, add flour and cook a minute until foaming. Add broccoli and stir until heated. Season with salt and pepper and add cream last. This makes only a small quantity but it is quite rich. It can easily be doubled.

Onion and Tomato Soup Beaureconne (see p. 100)

Broccoli Croquettes

500 g (1 lb) broccoli (out of season, this dish can be made using one 282 g (9 oz) packet of frozen broccoli).

Trim and use mostly the tops for the croquettes. Cook until tender in salted water. Chop the broccoli up very finely.

**60 g (2 oz) butter
1 white onion, finely diced
3 tablespoons plain flour
¼ cup cream
¼ teaspoon salt
pepper
1 large egg**

Melt butter, add onion and sauté until softened. Add plain flour and cook a moment. Add cream and stir until thickened. Mix in broccoli. Remove from the heat, season with salt and pepper and bind with the egg. Spread out on a plate, refrigerate and leave to set.

To Cook
**plain flour, seasoned
1 large egg
breadcrumbs, made from stale bread
2 tablespoons oil
30 g (1 oz) butter**

Take a small handful of the broccoli mixture, roll in flour, then egg and lastly breadcrumbs, forming small flat circles. Put aside to chill if not cooking immediately. It makes about 12, 5 cm (2 inch) across. Heat oil and butter and when very hot, cook the croquettes until golden and heated through, turning once. Serve with ham for a light luncheon or with a plain meat dish. The flavour of these is very light and delicate.

Spinach

This edible green would be the finest of the leafy vegetables, giving flavour to soups, soufflés, pasta, fillings. It has been served mostly overcooked through the years, boiled furiously and then presented in this unappetising state. Part of this treatment may lie in the old belief that raw vegetables were unhealthy and became edible only by long cooking and in earlier times, the English were particularly suspicious of raw greens. It was mashed and mangled and boiled beyond all recognition.

Some of the later popularity belongs to Popeye the Sailor, who was the creation of the late E. C. Segar. Originally a coward, Popeye soon became a fighter whose tremendous strength came principally from the spinach he ate by the tinful. Through this original cartoon feature, spinach consumption rose by an incredible 33%.

BASIC METHOD OF COOKING: Depending on appetites, 2 bunches of spinach is usually enough for 6 people. Remove the stems and discard any wilted or yellow leaves. Wash the spinach several times in a large quantity of water and drain. Place into a large pot with ½ teaspoon salt, leaving just the water that hangs on the leaf. Put on the lid and cook rapidly until just tender. Stir once, drain and run cold water through it. Drain again and squeeze to remove as much water as possible. Either chop or put through a *moulin* and leave ready for reheating in a little butter.

Spinach Mould with Sauce Polonaise

Serves 8

2 bunches spinach
½ teaspoon nutmeg
¼ teaspoon tabasco
60 g (2 oz) butter, cut in tiny pieces
2 tablespoons cream
2 tablespoons breadcrumbs (made from stale bread
60 g (2 oz) finely chopped or grated gruyère cheese
little salt
white pepper
¼ teaspoon sugar
3 eggs

Wash the spinach well and cook with just the water which clings to the leaves and a little salt until tender. Drain well and put through a *moulin* or blend. There should be about 2½ cups. If you find this too much trouble use the equivalent of cooked frozen spinach.

Place the spinach in a large bowl and add all the remaining ingredients. Mix well. It can be left like this and refrigerated for several hours before using. Stir again before turning into a mould.

Line a ring tin with butter and to make it easier to turn out you can also place a circle of foil on the base. Pour spinach into this, bake in moderate oven, 180-190°C (350-375°F), for about 25-30 minutes. Turn out carefully and serve with Sauce Polonaise.

Sauce Polonaise
2 hard boiled eggs
1 tablespoon lemon juice
60 g (2 oz) butter
2 tablespoons cream
little salt and pepper
2 tablespoons finely diced ham

Mash the eggs well. Mix with lemon juice. Melt butter, add cream and then eggs, and a little salt and pepper. Warm for just a moment and stir in ham
Don't boil the sauce.

Savoury Spinach Roll

To Prepare Tin: Butter a Swiss roll tin, line with greaseproof paper and butter this again. Sprinkle a layer of fresh breadcrumbs over the paper and shake away the excess.

1 bunch spinach

Wash spinach well and cook until tender. Drain. Chop very finely or sieve. Altogether about 1 cup of cooked spinach is needed for the dish.
As a substitute a 283 g (9 oz) packet of frozen spinach can be used.

60 g (2 oz) butter
4 tablespoons plain flour
1 cup milk
½ teaspoon salt and a little pepper
1 teaspoon dry English-style mustard
3 egg yolks
4 egg whites.

Melt butter and add flour. Cook until foaming. Add milk, salt and pepper and cook, stirring continuously until thickened. Season with mustard. Leave to cool for a few minutes. Add egg yolks one at a time and then spinach. Stir well. Beat egg whites until stiff and gently fold through a third at a time. Pour into tin. Bake for

15 minutes in a moderate oven, 180-190°C (350-375°F). Turn out onto a cloth or tea towel and peel away the paper.
Spread filling over the roll and using the cloth as a lever roll it up. Serve cut in thick slices.

Filling
30 g (1 oz) butter
1 diced white onion
125 g (4 oz) finely diced ham
1 tablespoon mayonnaise
1 tablespoon cream
salt and pepper

Melt butter, cook onion until soft. Add to ham with mayonnaise, cream and season with salt and pepper. This filling can be made beforehand as the warmth of the spinach roll is sufficient to soften it down.

NOTE: Although ideally this should be served immediately after cooking, if you feel this is a little complicated for last minute preparation it is possible to reheat the roll.
When rolling it up turn onto a heat proof platter. As soon as it is cool, lightly cover with foil. Reheat in a moderate oven, 180-190°C (350-375°F), for about 25 minutes or until warmed through.
Remove foil and serve. The roll may be served with a jug of melted butter if you wish.

Spinach Salad

½ bunch very fresh spinach
juice of 1 lemon
2 slices bacon
1 thick slice white bread
1 clove garlic
2 hard boiled eggs

Remove the stalks from the spinach and wash well. Leave to soak in a little water with the juice of a lemon. Drain and chill until crisp. If the leaves are extra large, they can be torn into bite-sized pieces. Cut the bacon into small pieces and fry until crisp. Remove and cool. Fry the bread in the bacon fat until brown. Cut the garlic clove so it has a flat end and rub over the bread while it is hot. Cut into small dice and cool. Chop egg up roughly. Place spinach in large bowl; sprinkle over the bacon, bread and eggs.
Add enough French dressing to moisten. Toss and serve immediately.

ROOT VEGETABLES

Carrots

Probably one of the main reasons so many people shun carrots it that they are so often prepared indifferently, especially in restaurants where as one of the three traditional tasteless vegetables that accompany the main course, they are boiled to death, and yet amazingly still mostly keep a bright good colour. At best, they are sweet and perfumed, delicately flavoured, a glorious colour and relatively cheap. What more could you ask of any vegetable?

BASIC METHOD OF COOKING: The large older carrots have a richer stronger flavour; the small baby carrots are lighter and more delicate. If using the larger ones. Trim and scrape with a vegetable peeler and slice across into thin slices. The tiny ones are trimmed and scraped and then either left whole or cut into long thin strips.

Place in a saucepan with 1 cup water, a tiny piece of butter the size of an almond, ¼ teaspoon salt, little pepper, 2 teaspoons sugar. Place the carrots in this (the quantity is enough for 500 g (1 lb) carrots). Cover and cook gently until the carrots are tender. They can be prepared beforehand and gently reheated.

Carrot Purée

500 g (1 lb) carrots
500 g (1 lb) potatoes
60 g (2 oz) butter
¼ cup cream
salt and pepper
little finely chopped parsley or chives

Cook the carrots until tender. Cook the peeled potatoes until tender. Put them both through a *moulin* or in a blender until a smooth purée. Add the butter while the purée is warm, then cream and beat with a wooden spoon until very smooth. Season to taste. If it goes a bit cool while you are doing this, then you can warm it agin in a saucepan. Mound on a plate and sprinkle the top, if you wish, with finely chopped parsley.

This purée is a delicate pinky colour and has a delicious buttery taste which lifts the flavour of the carrots from ordinary to superb. If you would like a stronger carrot taste, use 250 g (½ lb) of potatoes instead of 500 g (1 lb).

Carrots in Wine Sauce

60 g (2 oz) butter
6 medium-sized carrots, peeled, cut in thin slices
1 bunch spring onions, each one cut in about 3 pieces
¼ teaspoon salt
black pepper
a couple of pinches of cayenne pepper
1 teaspoon sugar
2 teaspoons sultanas
¼ cup dry white wine
¼ cup water
3 tablespoons cream

Melt the butter; add carrots and spring onions. Cook over medium heat, stirring occasionally for about 5 minutes or until a deep golden colour. Add salt, pepper, cayenne, sugar, sultanas, wine and water. Cover and cook over low heat until carrots and onions are quite tender. Uncover and turn up heat, boil until the liquid is just a glaze. Add cream and shake gently until hot. This dish can be prepared beforehand and reheated.

Swiss Carrots

500 g (1 lb) carrots, sliced and cooked until tender
60 g (2 oz) butter
1 white onion, finely chopped
2 stalks celery, finely diced
3 tablespoons cream
30 g (1 oz) gruyère cheese, chopped in small pieces
little salt and pepper

Melt the butter and cook onion and celery until softened. Add the carrots to the pan and warm through, shaking gently.
Mix cream and cheese together. Pour over the top and leave over low heat until cheese has melted. Season with salt and pepper to taste.

Carrot Cream

500 g (1 lb) carrots
3 egg yolks
¼ cup cream
2 tablespoons finely chopped parsley
pinch salt
pepper

Cook the carrots according to the Basic Method. Beat yolks, cream, parsley with salt and pepper. Remove pan with carrots from the heat. Add eggs and shake over low heat until a thick creamy sauce. Do not let this boil. The carrots can be cooked beforehand, reheated and then the sauce just added at the last minute.

Parsnip

The parsnip suffers in general from a tremendous amount of prejudice, usually limited to appearing only baked around a roast or thrown into a pot of soup along with a medley of other vegetables. It is probably banned from most tables through careless cooking. While we possibly couldn't agree with the Elizabethan belief that 'the roote of the Parsenep hanged on the necke, doth helpe the swelling of the throte: and no venemous worme shall harme the person which weareth the roote about him', we can surely subscribe to the thought that cooked really well, it provides new taste flavours during the winter.

Glazed Parsnip

6 small parsnips
60 g (2 oz) butter
salt and pepper
1 tablespoon brown sugar
½ teaspoon dry, English-style mustard

Peel the parsnips and cut in slices or strips. Be sure to check the centre is not woody at all. If so, discard it. Melt the butter, add the pieces of parsnip, season with salt and pepper, cover and cook gently until the parsnip is tender. Transfer to a small ovenproof dish. Mix the brown sugar and mustard together. Sprinkle this over the top. This can be prepared to this stage beforehand and them baked later in the day. Bake in a moderate oven, 180-190°C (350-375°F), for about 20 minutes or until very brown and glazed. This is slightly sweet, but is excellent with ham, chicken or pork.

117

Parsnip Puff

Peel 4 large parsnips and cut into pieces. Cook in salted water until tender. Drain well, put through a *moulin* or blend until a purée.

60 g (2 oz) butter
3 tablespoons cream
¼ teaspoon nutmeg
1 egg
salt and pepper

While the purée is warm add the butter cut in small pieces, cream, nutmeg, egg and salt and pepper. Spoon into a buttered, ovenproof dish.

Topping
1 tablespoon breadcrumbs, made from stale bread
30 g (1 oz) melted butter

Sprinkle the breadcrumbs over the top, then lastly the melted butter. Reheat in moderate oven, 180-190°C (350-375°F), for 20 minutes. This can be prepared in the morning and reheated at dinner time.
The parsnips become very delicate in flavour when served this way.

POTATOES

We have A. A. Milne to thank for this insight into human nature: 'If a man really loves potatoes, he must be a pretty decent sort of fellow'. The connection escapes me, but any vegetable that can stand up to being served once a day without losing favour is rather incredible, and it has the ability to absorb flavours and yet still retain its own character.

The method of cooking potates is determined by starch content. When new they have little starch and cook up dry and firm in texture. Older potatoes with plenty of starch are suitable for baking, cooking up to a mealy and loose texture.

It is incredible that such an important food is so carelessly marketed. There are not enough varieties of potatoes here and often it is more a matter of luck that the right variety is used for the right dish as they are rarely labelled in any way.

It is possible to become tired of the same familiar mashed, boiled or baked, so here is a bit of inspiration to maintain interest.

Potatoes Boulangère

1 kg (2 lb) old potatoes
1 large white onion
salt and pepper
60 g (2 oz) butter
1 cup beef stock

Peel and slice the potatoes thinly. Slice the onion wafer thin also, and mix them together seasoning with a good sprinkle of salt and pepper. Spread in a shallow ovenproof dish. Cut the butter into tiny pieces and dot over the top. Add stock. Bake in moderate oven, 180-190°C (350-375°F), for about 1 hour or until potatoes are cooked and stock is absorbed.

Potatoes Baked with Garlic

6 medium to large, old potatoes
4 large cloves garlic, unpeeled but cut in half
1 bay leaf, broken in half
60 g (2 oz) butter
salt and pepper

Grease a shallow ovenproof dish. Peel the potatoes and cut each one into halves or quarters, depending on size. Place into dish with garlic cloves and bay leaf. Melt the butter and pour over the top; add plenty of salt and pepper and toss gently with a spoon and a fork. Bake in moderate oven, 180-190°C (350-375°F), covered with foil for 20 minutes, then uncover and bake a further 45 minutes to 1 hour. Toss potatoes once during this time. Remove garlic and bay leaf before serving.
Although it has 4 large cloves of garlic, the flavour of this dish is quite delicate.

Baked Potato Puff

5 medium to large old potatoes (about 1 kg or 2 lb)
125 g (4 oz) cottage cheese
2 teaspoons grated onion
½ teaspoon salt
a little white pepper
3 tablespoons cream
60 g (2 oz) butter
2 tablespoons grated tasty cheese

Cook the potatoes in salted water until soft. Drain and either mash well or put through a *moulin*. Beat the cottage cheese into this with grated onion, salt and pepper. Lastly mix in cream. Grease an ovenproof dish with butter (size about 8 cup) and spoon in the mixture. Melt the butter and pour over the top. Sprinkle on the grated tasty cheese. Can be done several hours beforehand to this stage. Reheat in moderate oven, 180-190°C (350-375°F), for about 25-30 minutes.

Potato Wedges

This can be prepared using new potatoes but is best if done with old ones.

6 potatoes
salt and pepper
a little paprika
60 g (2 oz) butter
½ cup grated tasty cheese

Peel the potatoes and cut each one into wedges rather like an apple. Place in a greased ovenproof dish. Sprinkle with salt and pepper and a little paprika. Melt the butter and pour over the top; toss gently. Sprinkle with grated cheese. Bake uncovered in moderate oven, 180-190°C (350-375°F), for about 45 minutes.
This potato dish goes well with chicken or grilled meats.

Crunchy Potato Slices

6 medium sized potatoes, cut in thick slices
60 g (2 oz) butter
1 small clove crushed garlic
2 tablespoons cornflake crumbs, crumpled into small pieces
pepper and salt

Butter a scone tray and melt butter and garlic together. Slice potatoes thickly and arrange on scone tray, placing them overlapping in layers. Sprinkle with pepper and salt. Pour butter over the top and sprinkle with crumbs. Bake 45 minutes to 1 hour in a moderate oven, 180-190°C (350-375°F).

Hungarian Potatoes

1 kg (2 lb) old potatoes, peeled
30 g (1 oz) butter
1 tablespoon vegetable oil
salt and pepper

Dice the peeled potatoes. Melt the butter and add the oil. Pour over the potatoes, add pepper and salt and toss together well. Place in baking dish or casserole and bake in moderate oven, 180-190°C (350-375°F), for about 1 hour or until potato is cooked.

Topping: This can be prepared beforehand. If it goes firm it doesn't matter.

45 g (1½ oz) butter
2 thinly sliced white onions
2 teaspoons paprika
2 tablespoons cream

Melt the butter. Cook the onion until softened and a light gold colour. Add the paprika and stir a moment. Then add cream and mix through off the heat. Spread this over the top of the cooked potato. Return to the oven for about 5 minutes.
This goes well with chicken and steak dishes.

Potato Mountain

1 kg (2 lb) old potatoes
60 g (2 oz) butter
¼ cup milk
1 egg
¼ teaspoon nutmeg
little white pepper
¼ teaspoon salt

Cook the potatoes in salted water until tender. Drain well and either mash or put through a *moulin*. While still hot add the butter cut in small pieces. Stir until the butter melts. Add the milk and mix through. Beat in egg, nutmeg, pepper and salt. Grease a shallow round ovenproof dish and spoon the potato in to form a dome shape.

Topping
3 tablespoons soft breadcrumbs
⅓ cup gruyère cheese grated
an additional 60 g (2 oz) butter

In a basin mix together the breadcrumbs and cheese. Melt the additional butter and stir through.
Sprinkle this over the top of the potato dome. This can be done several hours before serving. Bake in moderate oven, 180-190°C (350-375°F), until the top of the dome is a golden brown colour and the potato is well heated through (15 minutes).
It goes particularly well with meat dishes that have a gravy or sauce.

PASTA

This actually dates back to the ancient Romans whose equipment for making, cooking and serving the earliest forms of pasta is preserved in the museum at Pompeii. By the thirteenth century, various books mention macaroni and noodles.

Italy is the homeland of pasta — fettuccine, spaghetti, perciatelloni, zitoni, lasagne, etc., etc. — but to try the five or six hundred different shapes and types would take considerable stamina, ambition and, of course, added inches.

Fresh pasta should always be cooked in a very large saucepan in plenty of salted, boiling water. Don't be nervous that you will oversalt it as it always needs plenty. I usually add a dash of oil to the water which helps to prevent the strands all sticking together. When the water is at a full rolling boil, add the pasta, let it boil rapidly, and test often by fishing out a piece and biting it. It should be just firm; don't let it go soft and mushy. Drain in a colander, mix with sauce and serve. How much? This is difficult as it depends entirely on the person who is going to eat it — Finicky Fred or Greedy George — so it is really a matter for the cook.

Noodles with Egg and Bacon Sauce

This mixture makes enough to cover 250 g (½ lb) cooked noodles. Any variety of pasta can be used successfully.

60 g (2 oz) butter
2 rashers diced bacon
2 large eggs
1 crushed clove garlic
½ cup grated tasty cheese
½ cup cream

Melt the butter and cook bacon until the fat is clear. Add noodles and toss. Beat in a basin, eggs, garlic, cheese and cream. Pour over the hot noodles and mix over the heat only long enough for it to become a thick sauce. Don't overcook the egg or it becomes dry.

Tagliatelle with Chicken Sauce

250 g (½ lb) tagliatelle; buy the green variety if you can
30 g (1 oz) butter
1 large onion, diced finely
1 small tin Spanish pimentoes (200 g or 6½ oz)

Cook the tagliatelle in plenty of well-salted water until just tender and drain. Melt the butter and sauté the onions until soft but not brown. Add the pimento to the onion and mix this with the tagliatelle. Season with a little black pepper. Put into a buttered, shallow ovenproof dish.

PREPARATION OF CHICKEN: Put 1 small chicken (about 1 kg or 2 lb) (or use chicken pieces) in a pot. Cover with water, add 1 onion, parsley, a little salt and cook until tender. Cool in liquid. This can be done beforehand and left in the refrigerator but make sure the chicken is well covered with liquid so it doesn't dry out. Remove flesh and cut into bite-sized pieces. Keep the liquid.

Sauce
60 g (2 oz) butter
3 tablespoons flour
1 cup milk
1½ cups chicken stock
1 teaspoon dry, English-style mustard
30 g (1 oz) gruyère cheese, chopped
2 tablespoons finely grated parmesan cheese.

Melt the butter and add the flour, cook until foaming but not brown. Add the milk and stock and cook until thickened. Add mustard, pepper and salt, if necessary. Add gruyère cheese. Remove from the heat and stir until the cheese is melted. Lastly add the pieces of chicken and pour this over the top of the tagliatelle. Sprinkle about 2 tablespoons grated parmesan (or tasty cheese) over the top.
This can be prepared in the morning and then reheated later at dinner time. Reheat in moderate oven, 180-190°C (350-375°F), for 20-25 minutes.

Party Pasta

30 g (1 oz) butter
4 medium-sized tomatoes, skinned
½ teaspoon salt
pepper
1 teaspoon sugar
1 clove garlic, crushed
pinch mixed herbs
1 teaspoon chopped mint
½ cup tasty grated cheese
2 eggs
125 g (4 oz) ham, finely diced
250 g (½ lb) noodles or tagliatelle. (The nicest pasta for this is a thin tagliatelle, preferably the green variety if you can buy it. Otherwise a small noodle can be used.)

Melt the butter. Cut the tomatoes into rough pieces. Add to the pan with salt, pepper, sugar, garlic, herbs and mint and cook about 10 minutes or until a lightly thickened sauce. Don't overcook or it loses the fresh flavour. Remove from the heat and add cheese; stir until melted. Beat eggs and add to this with the ham. Cook the noodles or tagliatelle in a large pot of salted water and drain well. Butter a shallow ovenproof dish, 5 cup size. Mix the noodles with the tomato and egg mixture and pour into dish. Smooth the top evenly and pour sauce over this. This dish can be made 12 hours beforehand and reheated most successfully. Bake in moderate oven, 180-190°C (350-375°F), for 25-30 minutes until the filling is heated and the top is golden and bubbling.

Sauce
60 g (2 oz) butter
2 tablespoons plain flour
2 cups milk
salt and pepper
¼ teaspoon dry, English-style mustard
1 egg
4 tablespoons freshly grated parmesan cheese

Melt butter, add flour, and cook until just foaming without browning. Add milk and salt and pepper and mustard. Stir continuously until boiling. Leave a few minutes to cool. Add egg and pour over noodles. Sprinkle the cheese over the top.

Clam and Seafood Sauce for Pasta

Too often pasta with seafood sauce turns out to be rather disastrous because the sauce is heavy and the seafood tough. Either tinned minced clams or small baby clams are excellent to use in this sauce.

2 tablespoons oil
1 large white onion, finely chopped
2 cloves crushed garlic
2 large ripe tomatoes, peeled and diced
½ teaspoon salt
½ teaspoon sugar
black pepper
1 small tin clams (315 g or 10 oz)
125 g (4 oz) scallops
250 g (8 oz) cooked prawns
¼ cup finely chopped parsley
60 g (2 oz) butter

Heat the oil and cook onion and garlic until almost transparent. Add the tomatoes, salt, sugar and pepper. Drain the clams and keep the juice. Add juice to pan and cook for about 10 minutes. Remove the coral from the scallops and trim them, cut into thin slices. Shell and devein the prawns and cut up small. Add the scallop slices, clams and prawns and cook for only a couple of minutes. Add parsley and butter. Mix well. Cook 500 g (1 lb) spaghetti or tagliatelle and drain. Mix with sauce and serve.

Personally, I don't serve grated cheese with this; just some good bread.

VEAL

Australian veal has never been very highly thought of, and too often the buyer has been given a choice between fairly young and not so young beef.

A few years ago Denkavit veal was introduced in Australia, allowing the dams' milk to be sold while the farmers could still rear the calves on Denkavit, a high energy skim milk base. This style of calf has flesh which is firm and smooth, finely grained and of a delicate pink colour. It is the best quality veal of all and lends itself to a large variety of flavourings. If this is unobtainable, and it is still not so easily bought in all the shops, veal is especially good in June and July when the calves are at just the right age. Veal should be pale but can become rose to quite reddish as the calf ages.

New regulations which have just come into effect prohibit the normal removal of the skin of calves the day after killing. This is now removed whilst killing and unfortunately the flesh as a result becomes darker in colour. The veal quality is the same, but because of the new ruling it is a little more difficult for the shopper to judge veal.

Veal and Whisky

Even if you are not a keen whisky drinker, don't be put off by this combination. It is a very delicate dish and the strong alcohol taste vanishes when it is flamed, leaving just the flavour.

6 thin escalopes of veal, cut from the leg
salt and pepper
60 g (2 oz) butter
1 tablespoon light vegetable oil (not olive)
1 white onion, very finely chopped
1 cooking apple, peeled and chopped
¼ cup whisky
¼ cup cream

The veal should be fairly thin; if not, flatten out gently. It is important that good quality veal is used for this dish. Season both sides with salt and pepper. Heat the butter and oil until foaming and add the veal. Cook over a fairly high heat turning once until it has changed colour on both sides and is just tender. It should only take a couple of minutes. Remove to a platter and keep warm in a low oven. Add the onion and apple to the pan, turn down the heat slightly and stir until they are just softened. Heat the whisky and light; add to the pan. Make sure when you do this that it is not over too high a heat as it can flare up quite a bit. Shake gently until the flames die down. Add the cream and cook, stirring and scraping up the juices until it is a thick sauce. Transfer the meat to a platter, pour over the sauce and serve. Potatoes and a side salad are best, as extra vegetables on the plate tend to get all mixed up with this sauce.

This can be kept in a low oven, covered, for about 10 minutes without spoiling.

Veal Roll with Mushroom and Port Sauce

60 g (2 oz) butter
1 large white onion, finely chopped
125 g (4 oz) diced ham

Melt the butter and add the onion. Sauté until softened. Add the ham. Remove from the heat.

500 g (1 lb) finely minced veal
2 eggs
1 teaspoon salt
white pepper
1 cup cream
1 tablespoon Worcestershire sauce

Beat the veal and add the eggs one at a time. It's much easier if you have an electric mixer. Add salt, pepper and then very gradually beat in the cream and Worcestershire sauce. Fold in the cooked onion and ham. Spread out a long sheet of foil and oil the surface lightly with vegetable oil. Place the soft veal mixture on this. Then roll up the foil to form a sausage shape. Turn the foil over and screw the ends up like a bon bon. As the veal is quite heavy I usually wrap this again in another piece of foil. Place some boiling water in a baking tin and put in the roll. Cook in the centre of a moderate oven, 180-190°C (350-375°F), for 50 minutes. Serve cut in thick slices with Mushroom and Port Sauce.

Mushroom and Port Sauce
60 g (2 oz) butter
125 g (4 oz) small mushrooms, or large ones cut in half
salt and pepper
2 tablespoons brandy
3 tablespoons port
2 teaspoons cornflour
1 cup cream

Melt the butter and add the mushrooms. Cook until softened, seasoning with salt and pepper. Add brandy and light, add port and cook the mixture gently for a few minutes. Mix the cornflour and cream together and add this. Stir until thickened. Taste and reheat as needed.

Epicurean Veal

60 g (2 oz) butter
¼ bunch spring onions roughly chopped
125 g (4 oz) mushrooms, sliced thinly
250 g (½ lb) ham, finely diced
1 large egg
2 tablespoons breadcrumbs, made from stale bread
salt and pepper
6 thin slices leg veal
6 small squares gruyère cheese

To Finish
plain flour
1 large egg, beaten with 1 tablespoon water and 1 tablespoon oil
breadcrumbs

Melt butter, add spring onions and cook a couple of minutes, add mushrooms and sauté until softened. Place ham, egg and breadcrumbs in basin; add mushroom mixture and season with a little pepper. Don't use salt as the ham will be salty enough. Flatten the veal lightly, season the veal pieces with salt and pepper. Place a spoonful of filling on one side of veal, then a piece of cheese on top. Fold over and press down gently. If necessary toothpick the edges together. Chill a few minutes

until firm. Dip the veal in flour, then egg and finally breadcrumbs. Sometimes it is necessary to use more than 1 egg, this depends on the size of the pieces of veal.
Keep refrigerated until dinner time. They keep about 12 hours like this without spoiling.

To Cook
45 g (1½ oz) butter
2 tablespoons oil

Heat the butter and oil and when very hot add the veal. Cook over a fairly high heat until it is golden brown and cooked through. If preferred the veal can be browned first and then transferred to a moderate oven, 180-190°C (350-375°F), for about 10 minutes or until cooked through and tender.
This is best accompanied by a green vegetable and a potato dish.

PORK

One of the advantages of pork is that served hot in winter it is a hearty and satisfying dish, while served cold in the warmer weather, the meat tastes delicate without losing flavour.

Until recently, winter pork was fattier but now it is mostly being grain fed and control is much tighter. The tendency in breeding is to cut down on the fat content. As a result, the meat is not quite so lavishly fat-streaked and marbled as formerly. The pigs often are reared under cover and in very modern conditions, so the meat does not vary greatly in quality from season to season.

It has always carried the stigma of trichinosis and people mostly overcooked it to death. However, it has now been established that after pork reaches in internal temperature of approx. 75°C (160°F), it is perfectly safe, instead of the higher temperature of 85°C (185°F) which was once often advocated. The following pork dishes are typical winter fare, warming, satisfying and very tasty.

Crown Roast of Pork	**1 crown roast of pork**

Stuffing
1½ cups breadcrumbs
¼ cup milk
1 teaspoon thyme
1 diced white onion
60 g (2 oz) butter
250 g (½ lb) veal, minced
1 teaspoon salt
pepper
1 cubed eating apple
1 stalk diced celery
1 tablespoon sultanas
1 tablespoon cranberries
1 egg

Mix breadcrumbs with milk and thyme and beat. Sauté onion in butter and add to crumbs with veal, salt, pepper, apple, celery and sultanas. Stir through cranberries and egg. Cover the bones of the roast with foil and put an empty tin in the centre so it will keep a good shape. Bake in a moderate oven, 180-190°C (350-375°F), for 30-40 minutes. Remove tin and fill with stuffing. Cook about another hour or until ready.
Serve with extra cranberries or apple sauce.

Pork Chops with Fruit Stuffing

6 pork chops.
Don't buy the very thin ones that butchers usually cut, but get them about double thickness. Trim away the rind and some of the fat.

Stuffing
45 g (1½ oz) pine nuts (can be bought in delicatessens or health food shops)
30 g (1 oz) butter
1 diced white onion, finely chopped
1 cooking apple, peeled, cored and chopped
½ cup breadcrumbs made from stale bread
little salt and pepper
1 large egg
8 prunes, stones removed, diced

Warm the pine nuts in a pan until they are golden on the outside. Remove to a large bowl. Add butter to the pan and cook the onion and apple until softened. Add to the pine nuts with breadcrumbs, seasoning, egg and prunes and stir well.
Using a very sharp knife cut a pocket in the side of the pork chops and season this. Fill with the stuffing and fold together. Place a wooden toothpick through the side and tuck the tail end of the chop up. This can also be held in place with a toothpick to make a tidy shape.

To Cook
1 tablespoon oil
15 g (½ oz) butter
1 tablespoon white wine
salt and pepper

Heat the oil and butter in a frying pan. Brown the chops on both sides. Transfer to a casserole with a lid, packing them together in one layer. Sprinkle the top with the white wine and then season with a little salt and pepper. Cover. Bake in moderate oven, 180-190ºC (350-375ºF), for about 30 minutes or until quite tender. The timing depends a little on the thickness of the pork but don't overcook or the chops will dry out. Remove toothpick before serving.
These can be accompanied by a bowl of cooked apple and some mustard if you wish. It is quite rich so a salad and plain potato dish goes best.

Pork Chops in Mustard Cream

6 thick pork chops
a little plain flour, seasoned with salt and pepper
30 g (1 oz) butter
1 tablespoon oil
2 large onions, diced
1 clove garlic, crushed
1 tablespoon white wine vinegar
1 bay leaf
1 tablespoon French mustard
½ cup cream
1 teaspoon lemon juice

Remove the rind and almost all the fat from the pork chops. Dip in the flour and shake away excess. Heat the butter and oil in a frying pan. When foaming add the chops and cook until golden, on both sides. Remove and place in a shallow casserole. Add the onions to the pan and cook until golden; add garlic and then the vinegar. Stir well to get up all the brown bits from the bottom of the pan and pour these juices over the chops. Top with a bay leaf, cover tightly and cook in moderate oven, 180-190°C (350-375°F), about 30 minutes, or until the chops are tender. Turn them over once during this time. Remove chops, skin away the excess fat from the surface of the juice. In a small bowl mix together cream and French mustard. Add to the casserole. Replace chops and warm them through again. Keep warm in the oven. Before serving, add the lemon juice.

Stuffed Pork Fillets

2 large pork fillets or 4 small ones (altogether you need about 1 kg or 2 lb of pork fillets)
60 g (2 oz) butter
1 large white onion, finely diced
250 g (½ lb) finely minced pork
2 tablespoons finely chopped parsley
pinch dried sage, or ½ teaspoon fresh, chopped finely
1 cup breadcrumbs (made from stale bread)
2 large eggs
½ teaspoon salt
black pepper

Trim the fat and sinew from the pork fillets. Cut through the centre and spread out to make a large piece. Flatten between paper using either a rolling pin or meat mallet.
Filling: Melt butter, cook onion until softened. Place into a bowl with the minced pork, parsley, sage, breadcrumbs, eggs, salt and pepper. Mix well. Cover 1 fillet with this filling; top with another fillet, rather like making a sandwich. Tie securely to hold together.
This can be prepared several hours beforehand.

To Cook
30 g (1 oz) butter
1 tablespoon vegetable oil
1 small white onion, finely diced
1 small cooking apple, finely chopped
1 teaspoon curry powder
1 cup chicken stock

Heat the butter and oil and brown the stuffed fillets on both sides, remove. Add onion and apple and sauté until softened; add curry and fry a minute, then add stock. Return fillet to the pan, cover and cook until tender. This takes about 1 hour but mainly depends on the size of the fillets.
To Serve: Remove the fillets, strain the sauce. It gets small pieces of the meat throughout, tastes nice, but looks messy unless strained. If you wish it can be thickened lightly. To do this, mix 2 teaspoons cornflour with 1 tablespoon cream and stir into the liquid.
Serve the pork (string bits removed) cut in thick slices with some of the sauce over each slice. It is quite rich so goes best with plain vegetables and salad.

OTHER WINTER MEATS

A collection of some winter dishes, slowly cooked, rich in flavour and aroma, and comforting dishes for the chillier months.

Lamb and Noodle Casserole

60 g (2 oz) butter
500 g (1 lb) finely minced lamb (not too much fat in this)
1 large white onion, finely chopped
1 clove garlic, crushed
3 ripe tomatoes, peeled
1 tablespoon tomato paste
½ teaspoon salt
black pepper
½ teaspoon cayenne pepper
1 teaspoon sugar
⅓ cup chopped green olives
125 g (4 oz) noodles

Melt half the butter and when foaming add lamb and cook, stirring until it has changed colour. Remove to a bowl. Add the remaining butter, onion and garlic and sauté until softened. Chop the tomatoes up into small pieces and add with tomato paste, salt, peppers, sugar and cook until a thick mixture (about 10 minutes). Remove from the heat, return meat and add olives and simmer another couple of minutes.

Cook the noodles (any type of noodle is suitable — provided it is not too large). Tagliatelle or a flat noodle is probably best. Break them into pieces rather than leaving in long strips before cooking). When cooked, drain and mix with the meat. Place this mixture into a buttered ovenproof casserole (about 10-14 cup size). Cover with cheese custard topping and bake 35-40 minutes in a moderate oven, 180-190°C (350-375°F), or until topping is golden and just set and lamb well heated through.

This is a good party dish; it can be doubled successfully and prepared 24 hours beforehand and be kept refrigerated until ready for baking.

Cheese Custard Topping
30 g (1 oz) butter
1 tablespoon flour
1 cup milk
1 cup lamb stock or a light stock such as chicken or veal
salt and pepper
½ teaspon dry English-style mustard
2 large eggs
250 g (½ lb) creamed cottage cheese

Melt the butter and add the flour; cook a moment until foaming and then add milk and stock. Cook stirring constantly until thickened, adding salt, pepper and mustard to taste. Beat the eggs in a bowl and gradually add the liquid. It will be rather a thin sauce at this stage. Mix with the eggs. Lastly add the cheese and stir until the mixture is quite smooth.

Braciola

4 slices bread, crusts removed
½ cup water
1 large egg
2 tablespoons parsley, finely chopped
1 teaspoon salt
pepper
1 clove garlic, crushed
750 g (1½ lb) finely minced beef

Break the bread into pieces and place in a large bowl. Add the water and beat with a fork. Add egg, parsley, salt, pepper and garlic. Add meat and mix well. Tear off a large piece of foil and brush the surface with a little water. Spread the meat on this in a shape rather like a Swiss roll. Over the meat place:

Crown Roast of Pork (see p. 125)

4 slices ham
2 tablespoons sultanas
1 white onion, finely chopped
3 tablespoons finely grated tasty cheese

Leave a small clear edge around, otherwise it is hard to roll up. Using the foil as a lever, roll over the meat to make a long sausage shape. Remember not to make it so long that it won't fit in your casserole. Press the edges together so none of the filling shows. Pinch this join with wet fingers. It can then be pushed up to a smaller, fatter shape if you wish. Chill in the foil for about 30 minutes for easier handling.

To Cook
1 small tin tomato purée (220 g or 7 oz)
or
1 small tin tomato soup (220 g or 7 oz)
1 tin water (use the purée or soup tin for this measure)

Place this in a casserole with a lid. Unwrap meat from foil and carefully tip into this. Place on a lid and cook in a moderate oven, 180-190°C (350-375°F), for about 1 hour. Baste the roll occasionally with the liquid. When cooked, leave to stand for 5 minutes. Remove carefully using a spatula. (The tomato mixture is purely to colour and flavour the outside and is not served with the meat.)
Serve the braciola cut in thick slices.
This can also be left to cool and served with salads in the summer. When cold it is possible to cut it quite thinly.

Beef Hot-Pot

30 g (1 oz) butter
1 tablespoon oil
1 large white onion, finely diced
1 green pepper, cut in strips
1 rasher bacon, cut small
500 g (1 lb) chuck steak
1 beef cube
½ cup water
1 teaspoon Worcestershire sauce
1 teaspoon brown sugar
½ teaspoon salt
little black pepper
1 teaspoon tabasco (this can be altered according to taste).
4 continental frankfurts
1 tin baked beans (454 g or about 1 lb)

Melt butter and oil. Add onion, pepper and bacon and cook until onion and pepper are softened. Turn up heat. Cut steak into bite-sized pieces and add. Brown, stirring in beef cube, water, Worcestershire sauce, brown sugar, salt and black pepper, and tabasco. Cover and cook until meat is tender (about 1½ hours). *Then before serving, cut frankfurts into chunky pieces and add; cook a minute, add beans and warm through.
The first part of the dish up to * can be prepared before hand, frankfurts and beans added just before serving.

Savoury Beef en Croûte

750 g (1½ lb) chuck steak
60 g (2 oz) butter
1 onion, chopped finely
black pepper
½ teaspoon salt
1 teaspoon tomato paste
1 beef cube
1 teaspoon Worcestershire sauce
2 tablespoons plain flour mixed with a little water

Topping
2 hard boiled eggs, chopped roughly
1 tablespoon parsley, finely chopped
125 g (4 oz) chopped mushroom, cooked in a little butter
salt and pepper

Trim the meat and cut into small pieces. Melt butter and cook onion until softened, turn up heat and add meat. Cook, stirring until it has changed colour. Add salt and pepper, tomato paste, beef cube, Worcestershire sauce. Cover and cook until meat is quite tender (about 1½ hours). Thicken with the flour and water. Remove from the heat and leave to cool. This part of the dish can be done the day beforehand.

To Finish
125 g (¼ lb) puff pastry
1 egg, lightly beaten, to glaze

Mix the ingredients for the topping, the egg, parsley and mushroom together.
Roll out the puff pastry thinly about the size of a Swiss roll tin. Place the cold meat down one side of the pastry. Flatten slightly and top with the egg, parsley and mushroom topping. Press down gently. Roll over pastry to enclose and tuck in ends. Glaze edges and top with beaten egg and decorate the top if you wish with cut outs. Chill. Bake in moderate oven, 180-190°C (350-375°F), about 30-35 minutes.
Serve cut in thick slices with sour cream sauce.

Sour Cream Sauce
½ cup sour cream
4 finely chopped spring onions
2 tablespoons sweet sour cucumber, finely chopped

Mix above ingredients together and keep chilled.

VARIATION: When making the topping for the beef add 1 dozen fresh oysters and then continue the recipe the same. The oysters mixed with the egg and mushroom give a superb yet delicate flavour.

Braised Beef in a Piece Bourguignonne Style

Braising is one of the most effective methods to tenderize meat. In most cases the standard practice is to brown the meat well before adding the liquids that form all the essential vapours, including varied seasonings. Probably one of the most universally favoured of all the braised beef dishes would be *Boeuf Bourguignonne*. The most usual method of cooking is to cut the beef into small cubes; the less common way is to braise it in one large piece. This is an interesting method as it keeps the meat moist and helps prevent it from overcooking. The cut of beef is of great importance. The long, slow cooking needed to produce a richly flavoured dish would reduce a tender piece of meat to shreds long before the stew was done. I like to use a large piece of buttock steak or else a cut such as sirloin or silverside (not corned). As cuts vary, the cooking times tend to differ. Testing after a certain time is the best way to determine when the meat is done. The size of the casserole or saucepan is important too; if too large and shallow, then you need to much liquid to immerse the meat adequately. Like most braised dishes, it is best when allowed to cool completely after cooking, the fat removed and then reheated the next day. This seems to mellow the flavourings.

2.5 kg to 3 kg (5-6 lb) piece of beef
a little plain flour
1 tablespoon oil
30 g (1 oz) butter
250 g (½ lb) speck (can be bought in most delicatessens)
2 tablespoons brandy
salt and pepper
1 large carrot, diced roughly
1 leek, diced roughly
1 large onion, diced roughly
2 cloves garlic, chopped
1 cup beef consomme
1 large bottle red wine (although quantity depends on size of casserole)
1 bouquet garnie of a bay leaf, fresh thyme and a few sprigs of parsley, all tied together with string.

To Finish the Dish
30 g (1 oz) butter
3 small button mushrooms for each person
salt and pepper
30 g (1 oz) butter
2 small whole white onions for each person
1 teaspoon sugar
2 tablespoons red wine

Tie the meat securely so it holds a good shape while it is cooking. Sprinkle with flour on all sides. Heat the oil and butter. Chop the speck into small pieces and add to the pan. Cook over high heat, stirring constantly until it has crisped and turned a golden brown. Remove to a bowl. Brown the meat on all sides in the same pan until a good even colour. Warm the brandy separately and light. Pour over the meat. Season with salt and pepper. Remove beef from the pan. If there isn't a thin film of oil on the base, add a little extra and then sauté the carrot, leek, onion and garlic until lightly coloured. Place the vegetables and speck in the base of a casserole or large saucepan and place the beef on top. Add consomme and enough wine to come almost to the top of the meat but not over it. Push the herb bouquet below the surface of the liquid and place a piece of buttered heavy paper on top. Cover tightly with a lid. Cook in a moderately slow oven, 150-160°C (300-325°F), or simmer on top of the stove until just tender. It can take 2½-3 hours but this depends on the beef. While this is cooking, prepare the mushrooms and onion. Heat the butter, remove stalks from mushrooms and add. Season with salt and pepper and cook over a good heat until lightly coloured but not soft. Remove. Heat the remaining butter in the same pan. Peel the onions, leaving whole and add. Cook over moderate heat shaking the pan from time to time so that they move round and brown on all sides. Sprinkle with the sugar and shake until lightly glazed. Add 2 tablespoons of red wine (or stock) to pan. Cover and cook over low heat until just barely tender. Remove and put aside.
To Serve: Heat the beef and add the mushrooms and onions to the sauce; warm them through for about 10 minutes. Check the dish for seasoning before serving.
If the sauce is too thin, make some *beurre manie* (small balls of flour and butter mixed together in about equal quantities) and add them to the sauce until sufficiently thickened. Transfer the beef to a heated platter with a slotted spoon, remove onion, mushrooms and arrange around the meat. Spoon a little sauce over to moisten and sprinkle with some finely chopped parsley. The beef is served cut in thickish slices. If you feel this is awkward to handle and keep hot, carve the beef and return to the casserole to keep warm, serving it then directly from the pot.

Rabbit

Rabbit is one of the poor relations of the kitchen, rather despised on most tables, despite its fresh and succulent flavour which teams well with mustards, white wine, onions and herbs. Unfortunately with the introduction of myxamatoses, people who may have once considered it on their menu are now even more doubtful. A pity because it has a lot more flavour than poultry and bought from a reliable shop the rabbits are carefully checked and selected. This is necessary as in Australia they are mostly all wild ones, and not especially bred for eating.

Marinated Rabbit with Prunes

1 large rabbit
1½ cups white wine
1 white onion, finely diced
1 medium-sized carrot, finely sliced
plain flour seasoned with salt and pepper
60 g (2 oz) butter
2 rashers bacon, diced
12 baby white onions
6 prunes
salt
couple of pinches cayenne pepper (or more depending on taste)
½ cup cream
1 tablespoon red current jelly

Cut the rabbit into pieces. Place in a china bowl and add the white wine, onion and carrot. Leave to marinade covered at room temperature for 12 hours, turning once or twice. Remove and pat rabbit dry. Turn in flour to coat lightly. Melt butter and add bacon and small onions. Cook gently until the bacon is crisp and the onions are glazed on all sides. It is necessary to shake the pan occasionally. Remove to a dish. Add rabbit pieces. If the pan is a bit dry, add a little extra piece of butter. Turn the rabbit until coloured on all sides. Replace bacon and onion. Strain the marinade over the rabbit, add salt and pepper, and place on a lid. Either cook over a low heat or bake in a moderate oven, 180-190°C (350-375°F), for 30 minutes. Remove the stones from the prunes. After 30 minutes, add to the pan or casserole. Continue cooking until the rabbit is tender. The sauce should be fairly thick. Add the cream and red currant jelly and shake gently until jelly is dissolved. This sauce has a slightly sweet and hot flavour. Because of this, the dish goes best with potatoes and salad or fried triangles of bread and salad.

WINTER PUDDINGS

The word pudding usually conjures up a picture of the old style suet or steamed pudding guaranteed to provide solid and substantial eating for even the hungriest of mortals. Winter puddings have altered in style considerably in the last few years. Most people have become more conscious of eating lightly, paying attention to the size of their waistline.
While these recipes are classified as puddings, they are still reasonably light and so can safely be served even after quite a large dinner.

Baked Jamaican Banana Pudding

30 g (1 oz) butter
3 tablespoons brown sugar
grated rind of 1 lemon
grated rind of 1 orange
5 medium-sized bananas (about 500 g or 1 lb)
1 tablespoon plain flour
2 tablespoons milk
1 large egg white

Cream the butter with the sugar, grated lemon and orange rinds until soft and fluffy. Mash the bananas. They need to be really well mashed or the texture of the pudding is not so nice. Add about half to the creamed mixture. Then sift in the plain flour and add the milk. Fold in the remaining banana. Beat the egg white until stiff and fold through last. (If you want a lighter pudding, use 2 egg whites instead of 1). Grease a baking dish (about 2½ cup size) and pour in mixture. It only makes a fairly small amount, but it goes a long way as it is rather filling and rich. Bake in a moderate oven, 180-190°C (350-375°F), about 25 minutes or until puffed and firm on top. Serve with Lemon Cream.

Lemon Cream
3 tablespoons castor sugar
2 tablespoons lemon juice
2 tablespoons white wine
1 tablespoon brandy
1 cup cream

Mix the castor sugar with the lemon juice. White wine and brandy. Whip the cream until stiff. Gradually whisk in the lemon mixture until fluffy. Keep chilled. This needs to be used within about 3 hours.
This lemon cream can also be served over fresh fruits such as strawberries or raspberries.

Peach Soufflé Omelette

1 large tin peaches, drained
1 tablespoon brandy
3 egg yolks
½ cup sugar
grated rind of 1 lemon
1 tablespoon lemon juice
4 egg whites
a little castor sugar

Cover the peaches with the brandy and leave to stand 1 hour, in base of buttered, shallow overproof dish (4 cup size). Beat egg yolks and sugar together until thick. Add lemon rind and juice. Beat the egg whites until very stiff but not dry and fold them carefully into the egg yolks. Pour the mixture over the peaches. Bake in a moderately hot oven, 190-200°C (375-400°F), for about 6 minutes. Sprinkle the top with a little castor sugar and cook another 6 minutes. It should be still creamy inside although it will go quite brown on top.

Chocolate Hazelnut Omelette Soufflé

First make the Hazelnut Praline

½ cup sugar
¼ cup water
½ cup finely chopped hazelnuts

Place sugar and water in a saucepan and shake pan slowly until the sugar is completely dissolved. Turn up the heat and cook until the syrup is a light golden colour. Never let it get too dark or it becomes bitter. Meantime, lightly oil a sponge tin or cake tin and sprinkle the chopped nuts on the base. Pour the toffee over this to form a thin layer. Leave to set. When firm, crack lightly all over and crush up. If thin, this is very easy to do. While not the traditional way to make a praline, this requires less work than watching the nuts and toffee cook together in the saucepan. Store in a sealed glass jar in the refrigerator. It keeps for some time.

2 tablespoons cocoa
¼ cup water
1 teaspoon instant coffee
4 egg yolks
½ cup sugar
5 egg whites
a little icing sugar

Mix cocoa and water together in a small pan. Cook stirring until thick. Add instant coffee and remove from the heat. Beat egg yolks and sugar until thick and lemon. Add cocoa mixture. (This can be done several hours beforehand.) Beat whites until stiff, fold in $1/_3$ at a time into chocolate mixture. Grease a shallow, ovenproof dish (preferably porcelain, about 4 cup size). Gently pour in half of the soufflé, sprinkle a thin layer of the hazelnut praline over the top, and then pour the remaining chocolate over this. Place in a moderate oven, 180-190°C (350-375°F), about 15-20 minutes. The centre should be still slightly creamy. Sprinkle the top lightly with icing sugar and serve. If you haven't used up all the praline, you can either keep it for the next soufflé or mix it into whipped cream or ice cream to serve with the dessert.

Baked Rice Pudding in a Caramel Mould

Line mould first.

½ cup sugar
¼ cup water

Place sugar and water in a saucepan and shake pan slowly until the sugar is completely dissolved. Turn up the heat and cook until the syrup turns a light golden colour. Remove from the heat immediately. Tip into the mould and turn until the sides are coated. Metal is easier to coat than china or porcelain and it is also easier to turn out. You can use either a sponge cake tin (20 cm or 8 inch) or even a long loaf tin is quite successful. Be careul though as the metal becomes quite hot while you are turning the caramel, so use a cloth to hold it. When completely coated and the caramel is no longer running, leave aside to set.

½ cup long grain rice
2 cups milk
⅓ cup sugar
grated rind of 1 large lemon
¼ cup sultanas
¼ teaspoon cinnamon
½ cup cream
2 eggs separated

Wash rice and place in a saucepan with the milk. Cook gently over a low heat until all the milk is absorbed and the rice is tender. Remove and add sugar, lemon rind, sultanas, cinnamon and cream. Add egg yolks one at a time. Beat whites until stiff and fold through. Turn this into the caramel lined mould. Stand in a dish of water and bake in a moderate oven, 180-190°C (350-375°F), until just set, about 25-30 minutes. Leave to stand for 10-15 minutes and turn out gently. Serve with unsweetened whipped cream. This goes well with a bowl of cooked pears.

ORANGES AND SOME OTHER WINTER FRUITS

Oranges

When Charles II pinched Nell Gwynn's cheek and she tossed him an orange, little was the pretty orange seller of Drury Lane to realise how this was to change her life. Although the Seville orange had been brought to England by the Portuguese, it wasn't particularly popular with the general public. When Charles began to show such an interest in Nell, the public, so easily swayed by such matters, elevated the fruit in their minds to be a symbol of love. And so they bought them and bought them, in fact in such quantities that eventually the poor were reduced to stealing if they wanted some of the expensive fruit. As always, all sorts of weird and curative powers were ascribed to the orange, people doubtlessly reasoning that anything tasting that good must also be good for you.

Reading through some old recipe books, I came across a recipe for an elixir of love which I pass on. I can't absolutely guarantee the results as testing is not yet completed on this. Make a powder out of half a teaspoon of sugar, 1 teaspoon of pepermint and 1 teaspoon of grated candied orange peel. Mix well. Give one teaspooon to the person you've set your heart on in a glass of wine and he (or she) will love you passionately and forever. You will find you have a little of the mixture over and this can be presented to any lovesick friends.

Orange Charlotte

1 cup orange juice
⅓ cup lemon juice
¾ cup sugar
1 tablespoon gelatine
2 tablespoons water
3 egg whites
1 cup cream

Mix orange and lemon juice together in a basin. Add sugar and stir until dissolved. Mix gelatine with cold water and stir. Stand over simmering water until clear and dissolved and add to orange juice. Leave until starting to thicken and set around the edge. Beat until very frothy. Beat egg whites until stiff and beat cream until lightly stiffened. Fold together and then fold into orange mixture. Pour into a large bowl and leave to set.

This dessert tastes delicious if set in orange shells. The charlotte picks up a light flavour from the inside of the shell. This mixture which makes quite a lot is enought to fill about 9 medium-sized oranges cut in halves. Remove all the fibrous part from the inside being careful not to break the skin. The shells can be kept in the freezer packed together if you wish ready for the dessert. Thaw and fill. If they won't balance easily place each one until set in a small patty case in the refrigerator. The top can be decorated with rosettes of cream and a dusting of chocolate or else a piped lattice of chocolate on top is effective.

Oranges Maria

6 large oranges
¾ cup sugar
3 tablespoons water
3 tablespoons lemon juice
few drops cochineal
1 tablespoon brandy (or more if you wish)

Peel oranges and carefully remove all segments so no membrane is left on them. Save the juice. Place them in a bowl. Boil sugar and water in a saucepan until it forms a thickish syrup. Remove and add the lemon juice and cochaneal, any juice from the oranges and pour over the segments. Chill and add brandy just before serving.

NOTE: Sometimes the amount of sugar may need adjusting. It depends on the sweetness of the oranges used.

Chocolate Oranges

This is a fairly time-consuming recipe, but well worth the trouble.

6 medium-sized oranges, remove the tops.

Remove pulp and all the membrane leaving a clean shell. Strain the juice.

Orange Ice Cream
½ cup orange juice
2 egg yolks
4 tablespoons sugar
½ teaspoon gelatine mixed with 1 tablespoon cold water
½ cup cream, lightly whipped

Heat the orange juice. Place egg yolks and sugar in a basin and beat until thick. Add orange juice. Stand this basin over a saucepan of hot water and cook, stirring until lightly thickened. This takes some time and if you find it a bit tedious place it all in a saucepan and cook over low heat stirring or whisking continuously until thickened. It takes only a couple of minutes this way but be careful not to let it boil. Remove from the heat, add the gelatine and stir until the gelatine is dissolved. When cold place in freezer and freeze until firm. Remove, break up, and beat well until fluffy. Fold through whipped cream. Half fill the orange shells with this and freeze until set. If they won't balance upright, place each one in a paper patty case.

Chocolate Ice Cream
85 g (about 3 oz) dark chocolate
½ teaspoon gelatine mixed with 1 tablespoon cold water
½ cup cream, lightly whipped

Break the chocolate into pieces, place on a plate and melt standing over a pan of hot water. Dissolve the gelatine and mix into chocolate. Fold into the cream. Place the chocolate on top of the orange ice cream in the shells and freeze. Cut across 3 times so they open out to form a flower, or else cut into sections and serve the sections on a platter.
They are best left a couple of minutes before eating as the flavour is best of they are not too hard.

Quinces

Years ago, when all the immortals were feasting, into their midst was flung a golden apple with the challenge 'For the fairest'. Thus began the quarrel which started the Trojan War. Aphrodite received it and since then, it was given the name, love apple. Legend has it that the love apple was the one which Eve gave to Adam. But nobody really can be sure except Adam. Nowadays it bears the unromantic name of quince. It was once prized, but is now a rather forgotten fruit, too hard to be eaten off the tree, but with a fragrant and incomparable flavour and glorious colour when cooked.

Persian Quinces

4 quinces
water
sugar
1 long strip of lemon peel
1 long strip of orange peel
½ cup sultanas
½ cup shredded almond slithers

Peel the quinces and cut into quarters. Core them and place in a large saucepan and just cover with water. Cook, covered, for about ¾ hour. Strain away the liquid and measure it. For every 2 cups water, add 1 cup sugar. Add the quinces to this with lemon and orange peels, and cook for another 30 minutes or until quite tender. Add the sultanas and cool. Remove orange and lemon peel when cold. Before serving, brown the almond slithers in a pan or bake on a tray in the oven. Sprinkle over the top of the quinces and serve very cold. They should be a glorious shade of red when they are cooked.

Compote of Rhubarb

Rhubarb cooked this way keeps its shape without breaking and has a lovely flavour.

500 g (1 lb) of rhubarb
juice of 1 orange
several strips of orange rind
¾ cup sugar

Wash the rhubarb and cut into pieces. Place in a double boiler. Add the orange juice, strips of orange rind and sugar. (Use a vegetable peeler to remove the rind from the orange and be careful there is no white on it or it will make the dish bitter.) Cook over boiling water until tender and serve either warm with cream, or else cool and serve chilled. Alternatively it can be cooked in a covered casserole in a moderate oven, 180-190°C (350-375°F), until just tender.

Festive

SAVOURIES

This is a selection of finger foods to go with pre-dinner drinks — choice little titbits, which have the ability to stimulate the appetite. Unfortunately the majority of savouries that are usually served are so predictable. While there is nothing really wrong with nuts, olives, crisps or cheese footballs, with the variety of foods possible to make, there is no excuse not to select a couple of dishes which are more alluring to the stomach and the eye.

Caviar Mousse

Serves 4

1 teaspoon gelatine
1 tablespoon water
1 tablespoon lemon juice
1 tablespoon mayonnaise
¼ teaspoon tabasco
½ cup sour cream
1 jar either black or red caviar (about 45 g or 1½ oz)

Soften gelatine and water and dissolve standing over hot water. Mix this with the lemon, mayonnaise and tabasco. Add to the sour cream. Stir well. Lastly gently mix in the caviar. Pour into a small container and chill until firm. This is served as a first course with hot buttered toast. Keeps well for 2 days.

Ham Cubes

6 thin square slices of ham (The packets of sliced ham are quite suitable for this dish)
1 125 g (4 oz) packet cream cheese
1 teaspoon mayonnaise
1 teaspoon horseradish
1 teaspoon Worcestershire sauce
pinch salt

Mash together cream cheese and mayonnaise, horseradish, Worcestershire sauce, salt. Place 1 slice of ham on a board, spread with filling, top with another slice, spread again and so on. When all is used press firmly to even out the filling between the slices. Chill wrapped in plastic wrap. Keeps 24 hours.
Serve cut in small cubes using a very sharp knife. Makes about 24, depending on the size. Put a toothpick through each cube and either serve plain or topped with a small piece of pineapple.

Sardine Pâté

1 tin good quality sardines (size about 125 g or 4 oz)
2 hard-boiled eggs
1 small white onion
1 tablespoon finely chopped parsley
1 tablespoon mayonnaise
cream if necessary to moisten
salt and pepper to taste

Mash sardines well, add eggs and mash together. Grate the onion into this, mix with parsley and mayonnaise. If not fairly moist add a little cream and then season to taste.
Press firmly into a small dish and chill. It can be kept covered for 24 hours in the refrigerator. Serve on toast or thin slices of buttered French breadstick.

VARIATION: The same method can be used with 1 small tin red salmon.

Steak Tartare Savoury

A great many people still can't come at the thought of eating raw meat but this savoury is a very well flavoured version of steak tartare and is eaten as a savoury spread. I must admit I rarely stress what it is until after most people have eaten; this way everybody is happy. And if you feel hesitant at trying this, just remember what it did for the Tartars. And if you're not sure what it did for the Tartars, try it on a tired gentleman friend one night.

500 g (1 lb) fillet steak, well trimmed of any fat and sinew
1 white onion, really finely chopped
2 teaspoons Worcestershire sauce
1 egg yolk
salt and pepper
½ small clove garlic, crushed
½ teaspoon dry, English-style mustard
2 teaspoons anchovy sauce
1 tablespoon lemon juice
1 teaspoon horseradish relish

The meat can either be scraped or minced. To scrape it, use a very sharp knife and scrape against the grain. It is really easier to mince it finely but it must be done only an hour or so before serving. Add to the meat all the remaining ingredients, tasting at the finish for seasoning. Keep well covered in the refrigerator.
To Serve: make into a large ball and serve with toast triangles. Or else use it as a first course at the dinner table and make into tiny patties, one for each guest. These are also surrounded with buttered triangles of toast.

Easy Liver Pâté

This is exactly what it states — a very easy liver pâté which can be made up quickly yet has a good flavour. It will keep for 48 hours.

3 rashers bacon
6 spring onions, finely chopped
250 g (½ lb) bought liverwurst
1 tablespoon dry sherry
60 g (2 oz) soft butter

Dice the bacon very small. Place in a frying pan and cook until the fat is transparent. Remove. Add the spring onions and cook in the bacon fat. Mash the liver, adding bacon and spring onions. Add sherry and butter and beat well. Usually it will be quite salty enough but you may need a little pepper. Pack into a small mould and chill. Turn out and serve with celery, extra spring onions and crusty bread.

Spiced Frankfurts

Serves 10

⅓ cup red currant jelly
2 teaspoons French mustard
1 teaspoon dry mustard
⅓ cup orange juice
20 cocktail frankfurts

Place jelly, mustards and orange juice in a saucepan and warm until the red currant jelly is melted. If the cocktail frankfurts are large ones, cut in half. Add to the sauce and cook gently for a few minutes. Remove and serve on toothpicks. They should have a lovely glaze on the outside. You need a plate for these when serving as they tend to be a bit on the drippy side. Drippy or not, they are a terrific hit with the men.

Savoury Bacon Puffs

Makes about 24 of these

250 g (½ lb) puff paste
1 egg beaten well
¾ cup lightly packed grated tasty cheese
1 large rasher bacon
a little French mustard
sesame seeds

Roll the puff pastry out thinly and cut out circles using a scone cutter. Brush half the circles with egg and put a little tasty cheese on top. Cut the bacon into small pieces; if very fatty don't use this part but trim away. Place a little of the bacon on top and then dot with a tiny bit of French mustard. Top with a second circle and press the edges together. Brush edges and top with egg. Sprinkle the top with sesame seeds. These are a bit tedious to make but can be prepared beforehand and refrigerated. They can also be frozen. Bake on a buttered scone tray in a moderately hot oven for about 5 to 6 minutes at 200-220°C (400-425°F). These make a very tasty savoury or else can be served as an accompaniment to a soup in the winter.

Prawn Rolls

Makes 20

Filling
2 large hard-boiled eggs
250 g (½ lb) prawns, shelled and chopped
3 shredded lettuce leaves (about ¾ cup, fairly firmly packed)
2 teaspoons mayonnaise
salt and pepper
½ teaspoon curry powder

Mash egg and mix in other ingredients. Must be well seasoned.

250 g (½ lb) puff pastry
1 egg to glaze

Roll out pastry very thinly. Cut into strips and put a little filling on each one (rather like making sausage rolls). Turn over to enclose filling. Brush top and edges with egg to seal the top. Prick once and chill. Can be kept 12 hours refrigerated at this stage. Bake in hot oven, 200-220°C (400-425°F), approximately 12 minutes or until pastry is puffed and golden.

Chicken Crescents

Makes approximately 12

Filling
1 cup cooked chicken
60 g (2 oz) soft butter
1 large hard-boiled egg
salt and pepper
1 tablespoon finely chopped parsley
good pinch thyme
125 g (4 oz) cooked sliced mushrooms
250 g (½ lb) puff pastry
1 egg for glazing

Chop chicken very finely (or mince) and mash with soft butter. Mash egg and add with salt and pepper, parsley, thyme and mushrooms.
Roll puff pastry out thinly and cut out small circles (about 10 cm or 4 inch in diameter). Put a little filling (about 2 teaspoons) on one side of each circle only, fold over like a pastie and press edges together. Glaze top and edges with beaten egg. Chill. They can be kept like this for 24 hours. Prick the top and cook on a buttered tray in a hot oven, 200-220°C (400-425°F), for 8-10 minutes.

Through modern methods and breeding, chicken has become one of the cheapest, most convenient and flavourless of foods. It is always very tender but needs the addition of flavourings and sauces and careful cooking to make it an exciting dish. I personally prefer fresh and not frozen birds and interesting stuffings can do a lot to liven up an ordinary roast chicken. While it is one of the most often used of all meats throughout the whole year poultry still has strong association with Christmas and all festive occasions.

CHICKEN, DUCK AND A TURKEY

Spiced Chicken Sweet Jade

Serves 8

2 chickens each about 1.5 kg (3 lb)

Marinade
½ cup red wine
2 tablespoons soy sauce
2 small strips fresh green ginger
2 chopped cloves garlic
2 tablespoons honey

Cut each chicken into quarters and place into a shallow dish. Heat the marinade ingredients and pour while still warm over chicken. Cool and then keep refrigerated 24 hours, turning several times.
To Bake: Place in shallow, ovenproof dish in one layer. Add enough of the marinade to just cover the base and then bake in moderate oven, 180-190°C (350-375°F), for about 1¼ hours. If the skin goes too dark cover the top of the dish loosely with foil, or if the dish becomes dry, spoon over a bit more marinade. This is a dish which can be kept warm for some time without spoiling. Serve with rice pilaff and salad.

Stuffed Chicken Legs

60 g (2 oz) butter
250 g (½ lb) mushrooms, sliced thinly
2 white onions, finely chopped
1 tablespoon port
pepper and salt
6 chicken legs, thighs attached
plain flour
little peanut oil
6 squares foil

Melt the butter; sauté mushrooms and onions until softened. Add port, seasonings and cook until reduced and thick. Leave to cool. Using your fingers separate the skin from the legs of the chicken being careful not to pierce it. Stuff with a little of the mushroom mixture pushing it in with a teaspoon or fingers. Press the skin back. This is quite easy. Rub the chicken with a little salt and pepper, oil and flour. Chill. Brush the foil squares with a little oil. Wrap 1 piece of chicken in each forming an airtight package. Keep refrigerated. Can be kept in refrigerator 12 hours like this. Bake in a moderate oven, 180-190°C (350-375°F), for 20 minutes, loosen the foil parcels and undo and leave open for another 20 minutes to brown. Serve each leg with a little of the juice from the foil.

Chicken Princess

Serves 8

2 small chickens, about 1.5 kg (3 lb) each or 1 large one

Place in a pot, breast side down, just barely cover with water, add salt, 1 roughly chopped onion, and a few parsley stalks. Cook, covered until tender. Leave to cool in the liquid, breast side down still, and when cold transfer to the refrigerator. Keep chilled in a basin, completely covered with the liquid. They can be cooked several days before using, and will stay moist and juicy if kept this way. When using remove all jelly from around the chickens and cut into portions. Place these in a shallow ungreased ovenproof dish in one layer. Cover with sauce and then keep refrigerated. It can be prepared to this stage 8 hours before. Bake in moderate oven, 180-190°C (350-375°F), for about 30 minutes.

This is a very good buffet dish as it's easy to prepare and serve. The chicken can be cooked several days beforehand and the sauce mixed and left for 24 hours in the refrigerator.

Sauce
30 g (1 oz) butter
125 g (4 oz) mushrooms
salt and pepper
¾ cup cream, whipped lightly
1 tablespoon Worcestershire sauce
2 teaspoons chopped paw paw and mango chutney
1 tablespoon mayonnaise
2 teaspoons French mustard
1 teaspoon dry mustard

Melt the butter and slice the mushrooms finely. Cook in the butter, adding a little salt and pepper until just softened. Leave to cool. Mix the cream and remaining ingredients in a bowl and add the cooled mushrooms.
This sauce is rather on the runny side and the dish goes well served with noodles and salad.

Weekend Chicken

Serves 4

This gets its name because the chicken can be prepared on a Friday and baked, and it is still moist and flavoursome to serve over the weekend. The pale green stuffing is inserted between the skin and the flesh of the chicken giving it a delicious taste and a crisp brown skin. It is a dish which is equally good hot or cold.

1 chicken, about 1.5 kg (3 lb)

Stuffing:
1 large white onion, very finely chopped
½ cup finely chopped parsley
1 tablespoon chopped fresh thyme or a little dried
2 large eggs
60 g (2 oz) melted butter
½ teaspoon salt
black pepper
1½ cups breadcrumbs made from stale white bread
1 tablespoon cream

Place onion, parsley, thyme, eggs, butter, salt and pepper in a bowl and beat. Add breadcrumbs and then cream. Insert your fingers inside the skin of the chicken, over the breast and then down the legs and carefully tear any connecting tissue. It's a bit messy but not difficult to do unless you have very sharp fingernails, in which case be careful not to tear the skin. Push the stuffing into this cavity, filling the skin around the leg first, then the breast so there is a thick layer of the green filling under the skin. Truss.

To Cook
30 g (1 oz) butter
salt and pepper
1 tablespoon vegetable oil

Melt the butter and brush the chicken breast and legs, using a pastry brush. Season lightly with salt and pepper. Place the oil in a baking tin and cook the chicken in a moderate oven, 180-190°C (350-375°F), for about 1½ hours or until tender. Turn during this cooking time and baste the breast and legs each time with the butter and juices in the pan. It is served without a gravy as a rule.

Chicken and Prawns

The province of Dauphine in France varies greatly in character from green fields and blue ribbons of river to a huge mass of mountains and the dishes also vary being either very simple or very rich. In this particular one the fields and river are combined to make an interesting combination of flavours. Instead of the small *ecrevisses* which are found in the rivers, medium-sized prawns can be used. The dish can be partly prepared several hours beforehand up to adding the prawns. These can be cooked and flamed in the brandy ready and then added later just at the last minute. If put in too long before, they will toughen.

Stage 1
1 large chicken
salt and pepper
60 g (2 oz) butter
2 cups white wine
2 large peeled and diced tomatoes

Cut chicken into portions and season with salt and pepper. Melt the butter and brown the chicken on all sides. Add 1 cup of the white wine, leave the lid off and cook over fairly high heat until most of the liquid is evaporated, turning the chicken occasionally. Add the second cup of wine and do the same. It should take about 30 minutes or even a bit longer. Add the tomatoes, cover and cook gently until the chicken is tender.

Stage 2
500 g (1 lb) prawns — raw are best; if you can't get them the cooked ones can be used
60 g (2 oz) butter
1 chopped shallot
1 clove crushed garlic
2 tablespoons brandy

Peel prawns but leave tail on — it helps them to stay in a good shape. Melt the butter, add shallots and garlic and cook 1 minute; add prawns and stir, then add brandy and light. Mix this into chicken.

Stage 3
2 tablespoons dry vermouth
2 tablespoons Madeira
1 tablespoon plain flour
½ cup cream

Mix dry vermouth, Madeira and plain flour with cream. Mix into chicken and shake gently to thicken. Taste for seasoning. Keep warm.

Stuffed Chicken Breasts

6 chicken breasts, boned out and skinned
seasoning of salt and pepper

Filling
30 g (1 oz) butter
1 large white onion, finely diced
60 g (2 oz) mushrooms, sliced (½ cup)
1 large tomato, skinned and chopped
1 tablespoon port
4 tablespoons fresh breadcrumbs
1 tablespoon finely chopped parsley
salt and pepper
1 egg

To Cook
60 g (2 oz) butter
½ cup white wine
½ cup chicken stock

Gently beat chicken breasts until very thin. Season with salt and pepper. Place a spoonful of stuffing on each and roll up, tucking in the ends. Then tie at each end.
To Prepare Filling: Melt butter and cook onion until softened. Add the mushroom; cook stirring; add fresh tomato and port. Cook 1 minute, then remove; add breadcrumbs, parsley, salt and pepper, and egg. Leave to cool (can be kept 24 hours).
To Cook: Melt the butter in a frying pan, add chicken and turn till golden on outside. Pour in wine and stock and simmer till tender, turning once. This should only take about 6 minutes.
Remove string before serving. Excellent with puréed spinach.

Almond Chicken Breasts

6 chicken breasts
1 cup milk
½ teaspoon curry powder
¼ teaspoon nutmeg
½ teaspoon salt
pepper
½ teaspoon dry English-style mustard
pinch mixed herbs
1 egg
2 teaspoons oil
plain flour, seasoned
equal quantity of breadcrumbs and finely chopped almonds (each chicken breast takes about 1 tablespoon of each)

Soak the chicken breasts in the milk mixed with curry powder, nutmeg, salt, pepper, mustard and mixed herbs. Leave in refrigerator for 24 hours. Drain. Beat the egg and oil. Dip the breasts in flour first, then egg, then breadcrumbs and almond mixture.

Heat in a Pan
2 tablespoons oil
30 g (1 oz) butter

Fry the chicken breasts until golden brown and tender. They should stay very moist. Don't overcook — breast of chicken should only take a few minutes both sides.
Serve immediately.

Swiss Chicken Breasts

6 chicken breasts
a little plain flour, seasoned with salt and pepper
60 g (2 oz) butter
1 tablespoon oil
6 circles of ham
an additional 30 g (1 oz) butter
6 medium-sized mushrooms, cut in thin slices
squeeze of lemon juice
6 circles of gruyère cheese

Remove the bones from the chicken breasts. Skin and flatten gently. Dip in the seasoned plain flour.

Melt the butter and oil and when foaming cook the chicken breasts 2-3 minutes on both sides over a medium heat. They should be cooked through as the second stage is mostly reheating. Place in a shallow, ovenproof dish. Top each one with a slice of ham, trimmed about the same size as the chicken. Melt the remaining butter and cook the mushrooms until softened (with salt, pepper and a squeeze of lemon juice). Spread a little of this on each of the chicken breasts. Top with cheese. Pour a thin layer of chicken stock into the base of an ovenproof dish. Place chicken breasts in this. Bake in moderate oven, 180-190°C (350-375°F), for about 10-12 minutes, or until chicken is heated and cheese is melted. Time really depends on the thinness of the chicken breast. Don't overcook or the cheese will melt away.

Roast Duckling with Apricot Sauce

1 duck about 1.5 kg (3 lb) or slightly larger
salt and pepper
1 white onion

Remove any loose fat from around the neck and the body cavity. Cut off the lower part of the wing. Prick the skin along the thighs, back and lower part of the breast. This helps to let the duck fat escape during the cooking. Season the cavity. Peel the onion and cut in quarters. Put inside duck and tie the bird, tucking the neck skin under to make a neat appearance. Place the duck in a roasting tin and place in the middle of a moderatly hot oven, 200-220°C (400-425°F), for about 15 minutes to brown lightly. Turn oven down to moderate, 180-190°C (350-375°F) and turn on its side. Drain away the fat occasionally. If necessary, carefully tip it out, but a bulb baster makes the job much easier. After another 30 minutes, turn on the other side. Cook until done. It should only take another 30 minutes or so, but this depends a lot on the duck. When ready remove trussing string, turn oven off, salt lightly and leave in the oven on a serving dish for a few minutes. It can rest 15 minutes like this.

Sauce
1 small tin apricot halves, 470 g (15 oz)
¼ cup Madeira
1 small piece glace ginger, finely chopped
couple of pinches cinnamon
1 tablespoon brandy
2 tablespoons curacao

Push the apricots through a *moulin* or sieve or blend. Add the Madeira, chopped ginger and cinnamon. Place in a small saucepan and cook gently for a few minutes, or until lightly thickened. This sauce can be made beforehand and reheated. Lastly, add the brandy and curaçao and serve hot with the duck.

1 duck, this size, will really only serve 4 people, as it has far more carcass and less meat than a chicken of corresponding weight. Remove the joints and drumsticks and then turn over. Remove the breast meat and cut into very thin slices.

Duck served with a fruit sauce doesn't really go very well with vegetables; rather just a platter of potatoes and a side salad.

Ballotine of Duckling

1 duck about 1.5 kg (3 lb) or slightly larger — boned

Unfortunately, the average person usually gets a mental block when reading 'first bone your duck'. This is a pity because it is not really difficult and shouldn't take much longer than cutting up 1 kg (2 lb) of meat for a casserole. It makes the serving of duck very simple — just a matter then of cutting straight through in slices. The main aim of the whole business is to detach the flesh and skin from the bones without breaking the skin, except for the cut at the back where the duck has to be first opened. Remember to always keep the cutting edge of the knife facing bone and not outside flesh. I find a small, very sharp and fine pointed knife the easiest to work with. Slit the duck along the back from the neck to the tail, exposing the backbone. Cut the skin and flesh away from the carcass down one side. When you come to the joints of the legs and wings which is very quickly, cut through the joint so that the leg and wing come away with the flesh. Continue cutting down until the ridge of the breast bone is reached. Be careful — the bone is very close to the skin here. Turn the duck and repeat on the other side. Cut very carefully along the ridge of the breast bone and take out the whole of the rib cage being careful not to slit the skin. By this time, it begins to look something like a giant frog and this is where the mental block can set in, but if you just keep cutting against the bone you can't go wrong. Chop off the wings at the first joint. Open the skin and scrape the flesh from the leg bones and wings so the bones can be pulled out, spread out on a board, flesh side up — pat yourself on the back — and the duck skin is now ready to stuff. (If you have made any cuts accidently in the skin, sew them up with a needle and thread.)

12 prunes
½ cup port
60 g (2 oz) butter
1 white onion, finely chopped
2 stalks celery, finely diced
1 cooking apple, peeled, diced finely
250 g (½ lb) finely minced veal
250 g (½ lb) finely minced pork (not too fatty)
2 leaves chopped sage or pinch dried
¼ cup finely chopped parsley
½ cup breadcrumbs made from stale bread
1 large egg
½ teaspoon salt
black pepper

Place prunes in a small bowl; warm port and pour over prunes. Leave to stand for several hours. Remove stones. Melt butter, sauté onion, celery and apple until softened. Place in a large bowl with minced veal and pork, sage, parsley, breadcrumbs and egg. Season with salt and pepper. Drain prunes and add port to stuffing. Mix well. Form half of the stuffing into a fat sausage shape. Flatten slightly. Arrange a line of prunes down the centre of it. Top with remaining stuffing. Shape and press together to form one roll. Place this on the duck skin and wrap the skin around it. Sew down the join. This is quite easy as the duck skin will be soft. Tie at intervals with string. Place on a rack in a baking dish and put into a moderate oven, 180-190°C (350-375°F). Leave for 15 minutes, prick the skin and then cook, turning occasionally. Altogether the duck should take about 1½ hours. During the cooking time, prick the skin occasionally to release the fat and also tip it away as it accumulates. Remove string. It can be served hot cut in thick slices with a little gravy or is delicious cold and then can be sliced very thinly.

Gravy
1 tablespoon flour
1 cup chicken or duck stock
1 tablespoon red currant jelly

Remove most of the fat from the pan and leave just a tablespoon. Add flour and cook over the heat until lightly coloured. Add stock and red currant jelly and stir until jelly is melted and sauce has thickened lightly. Serve in a jug with the duck.

Turkey Stuffed with Apples and Prunes

Serves 10-12

The stuffing in this recipe helps lubricate the bird as well as adding to the flavour.

3.5 kg-5 kg (7-10 lb) turkey
60 g-90 g (2-3 oz) butter

The day beforehand wash the turkey under cold, running water. Clear the cavity inside and dry well with paper towels inside and out. The stuffing can also be prepared and kept refrigerated the day before, but it is better not to stuff the turkey or else it may sweat inside.

Stuffing
500 g (1 lb) cooking apples
30 g (1 oz) butter
12 spring onions, roughly chopped
500 g (1 lb) pork, minced (include a little fat with it)
12 prunes
1 teaspoon salt
black pepper
2 cups soft white breadcrumbs
2 large beaten eggs

Peel and core the apples and place in a saucepan with 1 tablespoon water. Cover and cook, stirring occasionally until soft. Remove the lid and stir until a thick purée. Melt the butter, add spring onions, cook 1 minute, add pork and stir until cooked.

Pour boiling water over prunes, leave for about 10 minutes to plump, drain, remove stones. In a large basin, mix minced pork, apples, prunes, breadcrumbs, salt, pepper and eggs. Keep stuffing refrigerated, taking out about an hour before putting in the turkey or the filling will not do its work of lubricating the bird, as it will be so long before the heat penetrates to it. Spoon stuffing into cavity loosely. Sew up all the openings carefully with thread so no stuffing can escape or use small metal skewers. Rub all over with soft butter, sprinkle with pepper and salt. Roast on its side in a moderately slow oven, covering the top loosely with foil. Turn the turkey over at half time. Put on a heated platter and allow to stand for 20 minutes before carving.

Gravy
1 tablespoon plain flour
2 cups chicken stock
1 tablespoon Madeira
salt and pepper to taste

Pour off most of the fat, leaving just a couple of tablespoons in the pan. Add the flour and stir until smooth. Over low heat, cook, stirring, until flour is lightly browned. Gradually add stock, scraping up all the brown particles and sediment encrusting the bottom of the pan. Cook until gravy is lightly thickened. Add Madeira and season.

Timing for Turkey
3.5 kg-5 kg turkey requires 3-4 hours
5 kg-7 kg turkey requires 4-5 hours

A FEW CAKES

Slimmers should by-pass this little section altogether. The festive cakes are rich with butter, eggs, fruit or chocolate, but almost worth that little extra inch.

American Fruit Cake

250 g (½ lb) butter
1 cup sugar
5 eggs
375 g (¾ lb) chopped glace cherries
185 g (6 oz) chopped glace pineapple
½ cup sultanas
60 g (2 oz) blanched almonds
2 cups plain flour
½ teaspoon baking powder
grated rind of 1 orange
grated rind of 1 lemon
2 tablespoons rum

Cream the butter and sugar. Add the eggs one at a time. Beat well. Mix together cherries, pineapple, sultanas and blanched almonds. Sift ¼ cup of the plain flour into these and mix to coat thoroughly. Sift the remaining flour together with the baking powder into the creamed mixture and stir. Add the fruits, orange and lemon rind and lastly the rum.

Butter a deep, square cake tin, about 20 cm (8 inch). Fill with cake mixture and smoothe the top. Bake in moderately slow oven, 150-160°C (300-325°F), approximately 1½ hours.

Blackamoor's Nightcap

Serves 8

This is a cross between a cake and a pudding. It separates into two layers — a firm chocolate layer on the bottom and a lighter spongy layer on top.

125 g (4 oz) butter
½ cup sugar
5 large eggs, separated
125 g (4 oz) dark chocolate
125 g (4 oz) ground almonds
½ teaspoon vanilla essence
grated rind of 1 large lemon

Grease a deep round or square cake tin, 20 cm (8 inch) in size with a little butter. Sprinkle plain flour over the sides and base and shake away excess. Line the base with a piece of greaseproof paper and butter this.

Cream butter and sugar until light and fluffy. Add egg yolks one at a time. Grate the chocolate or put in a blender. Grating is better but very time consuming. Add chocolate to the creamed mixture and beat. Then add almonds, vanilla essence and lemon rind. Beat the egg whites until stiff. Fold in ⅓ first, then another, and finally the remainder. Pour the mixture into the prepared tin. Stand this in a baking tin of warm water, to come about half way up the mixture. Bake in a moderate oven, 180-190°C (350-375°F), for about 25 minutes. The top of the cake should be firm to touch. Remove and leave in the tin to cool. Turn out carefully and remove paper. Keep refrigerated.

To Serve
½ cup cream
1 tablespoon castor sugar
½ teaspoon vanilla essence

Whip the cream until stiff. Fold in sugar and vanilla and whisk for a moment. Spread this over the top of the cake and decorate with a little extra grated chocolate or chocolate rounds if you wish.

Chocolate Rounds
30 g (1 oz) chocolate
square of waxed paper

Break the chocolate into squares and melt on a plate over a saucepan of hot water. Using a teaspoon make small rounds on the wax paper. Chill until firm and remove. Keep refrigerated and use to decorate.

Index

Seafood Aurore	84
PUMPKIN	
Pumpkin Pancakes	74
PUREE	
Broccoli Purée	112
Carrot Purée	116
Pea Purée	11
QUINCES	
Persian Quinces	137
RABBIT	
Marinated Rabbit with Prunes	132
RASPBERRY	
Raspberry Baskets	58
Raspberry Brûlée	57
Raspberry Chocolate Cream Filling	58
Raspberry Nut Torte	59
Raspberry Summer Pudding	57
RED CABBAGE	
Red Cabbage Sweet Sour	111
RHUBARB	
Compote of Rhubarb	137
RICE	
Paprika Rice Stuffing	33
Rice Pudding in a Caramel Mound	134
ROSEMARY	
Rosemary Butter	31
SAGE	
Meat Balls with Sage	31
SALAD	
Bulgur Salad (Tabbooli Salad)	43
Cauliflower Salad with Tuna Sauce	41
Chinese Snow Peas	12
Egg-plant Salad	51
Endive & Orange Salad	108
Green Salad with French Dressing	41
Lettuce Salad with Mushroom Dressing	40
Moulded Seafood Salad	38
Potato Salad	42
Salad Gwendoline	43
Spinach Salad	115
Tomato & Egg Salad with Sardine Dressing	52
Tomato Rice Salad	41
Pineapple Rice Salad	44
Welsh Salad	43
Zucchini Salad	42
SALMON	
Cold Salmon Mousse	39
SAUCES	
Savoury	
Brandy Cream Sauce	7
Butter & Lemon Sauce	89
Cheese Sauce	109
Curried Cream Sauce	47
Devilled Sauce	17
Mushroom & Port Sauce	124
Mustard Sauce	109
Orange & Mint Sauce	19
Polonaise Sauce	114
Ravigote Sauce	39
Sour Cream Sauce	130
Spiced Jelly	17
Spiced Sauce	38
Tomato & Caper Sauce	80
Tomato Wine Sauce	79
Tuna Sauce	42
Vinaigrette à la Crème	7
Sweet	
Apricot Sauce	146
Chocolate Sauce	89
Gooseberry Sauce	26
Lemon Cream	133
Orange Sauce	73
Strawberry Cream	61
Strawberry Sauce	74
SAVOURIES	
Caviar Mousse	139
Chicken Crescents	141
Easy Liver Pâté	140
Ham Cubes	139
Prawn Rolls	141
Sardine Pâté	139
Savoury Bacon Puffs	141
Spiced Frankfurts	140
Steak Tartare Savoury	140
SCALLOPS	
Scallops in Chive Butter	29
Scallop Ravigote	39
SOUPS	
Iced	
Artichoke & Pea Soup	35
Chilled Chodlick	36

Paradise Soup	36
Snow Soup	35
Hot	
Broccoli Soup	112
Chicken Soup with mixed vegetables	100
Cream of Carrot & Tomato Soup	101
Hungarian Style Beef Soup	102
Lentil Soup	102
Mushroom Soup	101
Onion & Tomato Soup Beaureconne	100
Potage Paul	102
Seafood Chowder	103
SOUFFLES	
Pea Soufflé	11
Savoury Mushroom Soufflés	78
SPINACH	
Spinach — Basic method of cooking	113
Spinach Mould with Sauce Polonaise	114
Spinach Pancakes	75
Savoury Spinach Roll	114
Spinach Salad	115
SPROUTS	
Sprouts — Basic method of cooking	111
Sprouts in Curry Cream	112
STRAWBERRIES	
Angel Mousse	56
Chocolate Strawberry Delight	56
Coeur à la Crème	55
Glazed Strawberries	54
Strawberries in Caramel Sauce	55
Strawberries with Champagne Cream	54
Strawberry – Cream Cheese Tart	55
Strawberry Hope Sauce	54
STUFFING	
Paprika Rice Stuffing	33
TARRAGON	
Chicken Livers in Wine & Tarragon Sauce	32
TARTS & QUICHES	
Almond Tart	93
Apricot Almond Tart	63
Asparagus Tart	8
Gooseberry Meringue Tart	26
Leek Quiche	105
Strawberry & Cream Cheest Tart	55
TOMATO	
Baked Tomatoes with Breadcrumb Topping	53
Stuffed Tomato Cups	52
Tomatoes in Cream	53
Tomato & Egg Salad with Sardine Dressing	52
Tomato Rice Salad	41
TURKEY	
Turkey Stuffed with Apples & Prunes	148
VEAL	
Epicurean Veal	124
Veal Roll With Mushroom & Port Sauce	124
Veal & Whisky	123
WALNUTS	
Cheese Walnut Spread	90
Walnut Crêpes with Chocolate Sauce	89
Walnut Roll	90
WHITING	
Baked Fish Fillets with Tomato & Caper Sauce	80
Fish Fillets with Prawn Stuffing	81
Whiting Adele	82
ZUCCHINI	
Baked Zucchini Mould	14
Zucchini Salad	42
Zucchini with Tomato Topping	14